MUM'S THE WORD

A HANDBOOK FOR SEPARATING FAMILIES

KAREN VARNEY

Mum's the Word
© Karen Varney 2019

ISBN: 978-1-925833-96-6 (paperback)

 A catalogue record for this book is available from the National Library of Australia

Publishing Manager: Jason Smith
Lead Editor: Kristy Hoffman
Co-editor: Kay Jenkinson
Cover design: Karen Varney and Evie Lucas

Printed in Australia by Ocean Reeve Publishing
www.oceanreeve.com

Published by Karen Varney and Ocean Reeve Publishing

REEVE
PUBLISHING

For every person who has had the joy of raising a child
truly the hardest but most rewarding achievement in life.

TABLE OF CONTENTS

ACKNOWLEDGEMENTS

Thank you to my mum, Kay, for her guidance and support not only with this book but in life. What a woman!

To my husband, Chris, baby George, dad, sister, brother, friends and family.

MUMS: Angela, Cindy, Stephanie, Rae, Vashti, Popi, Amanda, Bronny, Annie, Fiona, Fiona B, Shannyn and Annemaree.

Thanks to: Paquita, Cammie, Clea, Sam B, Evie, Caroline, Joan, Kristine, Marg, Jan, Joanne and Jason.

Special Thanks to: The Honourable Alastair Nicholson AO RFD QC, Monica Blizzard, Naomi Halpern, Karen Finch, Melinda Nutting, Amanda Sillars, Tanya Lavan and Tanya Somerton.

FOREWORD

This book consists of a series of moving accounts by mothers, outlining appalling misuse of our family law system; legal incompetence and rapacity; insensitive case management; bureaucratic obstruction and delay; and an inability to recognise or control the activities of manipulative litigants—their former male partners—resulting in the tragic consequence of being permanently cut off from their children. Regrettably, the same stories could be told by a similar group of fathers.

As a former Chief Justice of the Family Court of Australia, this appals me. I recognise that family law is a fraught jurisdiction, where some behave terribly towards their former partners, but despite the best efforts of those managing the system, this will always happen. However, what should not happen is that the system contributes to the problem, as these accounts demonstrate it does.

Why have we reached this situation? There are many reasons and the following is a brief outline. First, I will describe the system that the Family Law Act (1975) replaced, because it is not often appreciated how bad it was. It was based upon the principles of the nineteenth century English Matrimonial Causes Act (1959), where findings of matrimonial fault, such as adultery and desertion, determined who was entitled to a divorce and the outcome of custody, access, and property settlement. It was administered by State Supreme Courts. The law differed to some extent in each Australian state and territory until 1959, when the Commonwealth Matrimonial Causes Act was passed. It made divorce law uniform throughout Australia and introduced a no-fault ground of separation, where parties had been separated for five years. Fault-based grounds such as adultery and desertion were also still available. The law remained productive of enormous injustice to parties and children, made worse by the very limited availability of legal aid. This effectively excluded much of the population, including most women, from access to the law.

The *Family Law Act* (1975) and the Family Court of Australia

The Family Law Act was introduced by the Whitlam Labor Government. It was farsighted and progressive legislation. It narrowly passed the Federal Parliament and set up the Family Court of Australia as a Federal Superior Court. "Fault" was abolished and the sole ground for divorce was twelve months' separation as evidence of irretrievable breakdown of the marriage. An application for divorce was no longer essential to proceedings for custody, access, and division of matrimonial property. A generous legal aid system was provided through the Australian Legal Aid office, a federal agency, which meant all parties had access to legal representation if required, including children. The Act and the court came into operation on January 1st 1976. Court staff included counsellors, who developed free services in relation to children's disputes, eventually enabling 60% or more of them to be resolved without litigation. Legally-trained registrars and deputy registrars developed sophisticated approaches to the settlement of property disputes and case management.

The Family Court is a court created under Chapter III of the Australian Constitution. It was staffed by specially selected judges who were required by the Act, by reason of training, experience and personality, to be suitable to deal with matters of family law[1] , a requirement not applicable to judges of what is now the Federal Circuit Court. Because the Family Court is a specialist Federal Superior Court of Record, its judgments are binding on inferior courts like the Federal Circuit Court, thus promoting consistency of approach in courts throughout Australia.

Appeals were originally heard by any three judges. This led to confusion and contradictory decisions. An Appeal Division of the Family Court was eventually created, including the Chief Justice and Deputy Chief Justice and such other judges as are assigned to the Division, who are usually assigned upon the basis of their suitability as appellate judges. A General Division was also created consisting of all other judges of the court. It became the first specialist appellate court dealing with family law appeals in the world, and has significantly affected development of the law in Australia and elsewhere. This introduced a regime of judge-made law in a similar way to other Australian superior courts. The law provides that there should be a majority of members of the appeal division sitting on any appeal. Appeal Division judges can also sit as trial judges sitting alone in appropriate cases.

Early years of the Family Court

When the Whitlam Government was replaced by the Fraser Government in late 1975, it was more supportive of a conservative Australian judiciary and legal profession, which then tended to treat family law as unworthy of serious consideration by a superior court. Under the new government, Family Court judges fell behind the terms and conditions of their Federal Court and State Supreme Court counterparts and the court was understaffed and treated much less generously than other courts. This in turn, made the recruitment of judges difficult. No court can operate efficiently in these circumstances, particularly when it has just been set up and feeling its way. The situation of the court was made worse by a series of attacks upon judges in New South Wales from 1980 to 1985, involving the murder of one judge, the wife of another, and an attempt to blow up the Parramatta Registry.

Renovation of the Family Court 1988-9

The response of the Hawke Government, which took office in 1983, was a more measured one, and after an inquiry the decision was taken to "renovate" the court, which then received more Government support. It was against this background that I became the court's second Chief Justice in February 1988. At that time, then Attorney General, Lionel Bowen, implemented legislation to raise the pay and conditions of judges of the Family Court to those of the Federal Court, made good judicial appointments and agreed to a new structure for the court's administration. These changes also led to the appointment of the court's first Chief Executive Officer and administrative independence for the court. A Deputy Chief Justice and Judicial Registrars were appointed. An important step was the extension of the court's jurisdiction to deal with issues relating to children of unmarried parents, which added volume and complexity to the court's workload, but was a necessary reform. These were substantial improvements, but the court continued to struggle because of the failure by successive governments to properly fund it, reductions in legal aid and by the fact that judges had to deal with every contested case, many of which should ideally have been heard quickly by decision-makers at the Magistrate Court level.

Requirements for a Successful Family Court

- In my experience it has proven to operate effectively, a Family Court needs:
- Skilled judicial and administrative leadership
- Adequate funding
- A first-class appeals division
- Enough skilled judges to deal with the workload of serious and difficult cases
- Priority given to urgent cases such as those involving child abuse, including sexual abuse and family violence
- Enough judicial personnel at Magistrate level to deal with the great volume of shorter and simpler cases in a speedy and efficient manner
- Registrars to case manage and conciliate/mediate all cases
- Skilled counsellors working within the system to help resolve children's cases
- A separate inhouse court mediation service
- Highly trained support staff
- A generous legal aid system
- A wide range of geographical locations
- Ability to service remote areas of Australia, involving the appointment of Aboriginal and Torres Strait Islander consultants
- A constant examination of procedures and practice designed to improve the performance of the court.

The Howard (Liberal National Party) Government 1996

While many of these requirements had been met by the time this government was elected in 1996, some had not, and problems commenced immediately thereafter.

The government made savage cuts to expenditure generally, including legal aid and an additional vindictive cut to the funds of the Family Court. This caused the dissolution of the court's voluntary counselling service, heavily reducing the court's capacity to resolve children's cases and struck a vital blow at the court as a unique institution, combining counselling and conciliation with adjudication. Since that time, conciliation and mediation have largely taken place outside the court system, usually by non-government organisations over whose activities the courts have no control.

The Federal Magistrate's Court (renamed the Federal Circuit Court)

The concept of a Magistrate's Court has always been understood to operate as a court of summary jurisdiction, to deal quickly with more minor matters that would otherwise clog the superior courts. It also acts as a filter to send on to the more serious cases to be determined by the superior courts.

By 1996, delays had begun to increase and at my request, the new government agreed to the appointment of Senior Registrars with extended powers to deal with this increase, which was highly successful in turning around delays. However, the government refused to continue to fund them and set up the Federal Magistrate's Court as a separate court with a separate administration, occupying the same buildings and with virtually the same jurisdiction as the Family Court. Instead of complementing the Family Court, it began to act as a competitor, conducting its own procedures, rather than adopting procedures designed to fit in with those of the Family Court. This quickly led to confusion, delays and, in many cases, additional costs. In addition, it failed to perform what should have been its primary function, which was to act as a court of summary jurisdiction to quickly dispose of less complex cases and refer the others to the judges of the Family Court. Another major problem in the Federal Circuit Court has been that all interim and final decisions are determined by a judge as no registrars are employed, further exacerbating delays and placing undue pressure upon its judges.

A review was later conducted under the Rudd-Gillard Government (2007-13) which recommended the merger of the two courts, with the magistrates no longer having jurisdiction similar to that of judges, but this did not proceed, largely because of opposition from the then magistrates, now judges.

The problems of the Federal Circuit Court and its ability to service its workload efficiently or fairly has been what appears to have been further exacerbated by a consistent policy of the government to frequently appoint people without family law experience, even though that is the bulk of its work. There were, of course, appointments of competent people with such experience, but not enough of them. It has been suggested that these other appointments have been made for political reasons, to reward government supporters. If so, this is grossly improper and damaging to the judiciary. The setting up and structure of this court has proved to be a disastrous decision. It seems likely that there has been a long-standing policy of the LNP Government since the time that former Senator Brandis became Attorney-General in 2013 to delay, or fail to appoint, new judges of the Family Court as judges retired. This had the effect of preventing the Family Court from dealing with its workload.

The obvious intention of this policy was to eventually enable the government to confer sole jurisdiction on the Federal Circuit Court to deal with all family law matters except appeals. Its judges have much worse terms and conditions of employment and this provided a cheaper alternative than the Family Court, which the government had never properly supported. This policy greatly exacerbated many of the problems described in this book, while at the same time giving the government an excuse to proceed with its plan to dissolve the Family Court because of its lack of performance.

In 2018, the Attorney General, Mr Christian Porter, announced that the government would abolish the Family Court's Appeal Division and remove appeals to the Federal Court, whose judges have little or no family law experience. At the same time, he also announced an intention not to appoint any more Family Court judges and to let the Court wither away as judges retired. The policies announced by Mr Porter were sought to be justified by self-serving "independent" reviews carried out by people with little or no court experience, who were critical of the Family Court's difficulties in dealing with its workload, but completely misunderstood the differing procedures of the two courts. Further, the government engaged in no consultations with the legal profession, which has since expressed almost unanimous opposition to its proposals, or with the judges of the Family Court, or other significant stake-holders. Faced with probable electoral defeat, the government has now devised a plan to rush its ill-considered family law "reforms" through the Parliament at its final sittings in April, prior to the May election. In doing so, it has apparently backtracked to some extent on the decisions announced by Mr Porter to abolish the Appeal Division of the Family Court and not to appoint more Family Court judges. It appears that it has reversed the first policy and also recently appointed two judges to the Family Court. These changes are obviously intended to allay concerns of independent senators about the proposals, but the reasoning of the government is far from clear and neither are its intentions. It seems markedly irresponsible to rush through this ill-considered legislation immediately prior to an election. Any changes to a long-established system should follow considerable study and consultation with all relevant persons and careful consideration at a political level.

Reductions in Legal Aid

Another feature of the policies of the Howard Government and its Conservative successors, has involved heavy cuts to legal aid for family law. This has led to increasing numbers of litigants becoming unrepresented, placing increased pressures on the courts and creating injustice and more lengthy delays, as is apparent from the accounts in this book. This is a core issue, because, for the adversary system to work, each side must have the opportunity to obtain adequate and inexpensive legal representation, which the designers of the Family Law Act intended. Without it, the system rapidly becomes chaotic, as has occurred here. This will continue to be the case unless action is taken to restore a proper family law legal aid system. I also consider, that court procedures should be changed to become less adversarial, and the parties less dependent upon lawyers. The presence of lawyers will remain important, but not as essential as it is now, and their role will be less combative.

In 2007, the Family Court published a Booklet, Finding a Better Way, which advocated for a less adversarial approach to the conduct of legal proceedings in family courts, which had been partially recognised in division 12A, part VII of the Family Law Act in the 2006 amendments to the Act. The virtue of such an approach is that it wrests control of the proceedings away from the lawyers and places it in the hands of the judges and litigants. Unfortunately, although this approach was successfully piloted in the Family Court, the family law system has failed to sufficiently take sufficient advantage of this initiative. The way that the current legislation is drafted is to make the adoption of less adversarial procedures optional, at the discretion of the judge. This should be amended to make such an approach mandatory. In my view, this would greatly remove pressure from the Legal Aid Commissions and produce far better outcomes, as the Family Court's initial use of these provisions amply demonstrated.

Conclusions

What came into operation in early 1976 was a specialist Superior Court with power to hear family cases and appeals and which had an in-house counselling service to deal with children's matters and advise the judiciary as to their best interests and safety. What the LNP Government apparently wants is a non-specialist inferior court, with appeals being heard by a non-specialist appellate court. Non-judicial services are (as has been longstanding practice) outsourced. The end results of this policy are likely to worsen the situation described in the accounts contained in this book.

The Federal Circuit Court is no longer exclusively a family court and meets none of the criteria that I have set out as required for an effective family court. It will not address the very real problems of children and parents with the little of what remains of a great initiative. It continues to have judges with family law experience, but now has many judges who lack it, and it will be unable to attract appointments from the highest level of the family law profession, because of its inferior status and conditions of employment.

Finally, there is another serious problem that will not go away, which is that child protection remains the province of the states and territories. The evils of this approach are graphically demonstrated in the case of "Sally" that is discussed in the book. It is an absurdity that different child protection regimes operate in different states and territories, or that Children's Court determinations override those of Federal Courts. Curiously, no effort has been made by any Federal or State and Territory Government to address this issue, despite the obvious difficulties created by this situation. An obvious solution would be for the states and territories to cede child protection jurisdiction to the Commonwealth to enable a national system of child protection to be developed within the family law system. This is not a novel approach and has been used with great effect in New Zealand. It is more than time that we followed them.

'This book is a significant indictment of the effect that poor decision making by successive governments has had and is an important contribution to the ongoing family law debate.'

The Honourable Alastair Nicholson, AO RFD QC

INTRODUCTION

In May 2013, a dad who was a corporate client of mine, poured his heart out, telling me of the anguish he felt not seeing his children, and the unfair way he had been treated by his ex-wife and our legal system. He described the process like being invisibly strangled; battling almost three years in court. He presumed our legal system would be equal, supporting both mums and dads, being able to equally give them both time to resolve and investigate her allegations to make sure his kids stayed in his life. He was desperate to be heard and to connect with other dads who may also be in his position. At first, I thought he was just a jilted father, until I did some digging and found these statistics: *261 divorce cases are lodged every day in our family court system, one in six Australian children don't live with their biological father, and a startling one in three children don't live with their father in the USA*[2] . But the most staggering statistic of all was, and still is, the amount of people who take their lives due to the absence of a parent or child.

I was then contacted by parents and advocate groups from countries such as Spain, India, Japan, England and the USA through my social media page. I couldn't believe this was a worldwide problem. I knew I had to dig deeper, so without hesitation, I poured my time and personal savings into creating a documentary titled *Dad*. The film was supported by two politicians and was shown in Canberra at the Parliament of Australia in mid-2015 as part of a Senate inquiry into our family law system. Although many politicians and media outlets agreed there was a problem, they and many of the mainstream related organisations failed to support the film, burying their head in the sand, admitting the 'rot' was too deep.

Ironically, I found the strongest supporters of the dads were mums who had endured the same ill fate; being falsely accused of harming their children and watching them slowly slip out of their lives. Reluctant to put their faces on camera, they asked me to create this book. They wished they had a book like this so they could understand what they were going through, how the system worked and to know they weren't alone.

I became close to one of the mums, 'Sally', and in 2016 I attended her annual Christmas party. When I arrived, Sally announced the opportunity to be interviewed. Two girls who had grown up with Sally's daughters asked if they could be. After their interview, I opened the door to find a queue of relatives and friends, all wanting to have their say. Wounds opened and tears flowed as they were finally allowed to tell someone how they felt.

This issue doesn't only affect immediate family, but friends, family friends, grandparents, neighbours, and related members of the community. I have also found this is not a gender issue. It's about mental health, education and family values combined with a broken, over-stretched legal system which needs urgent review by the people who work every day with the families, and by the family members who have witnessed the system first-hand, not by politicians who have no family law or mental health expertise. This is our hope, and as a person who has recently become a parent, I know now more than ever that all a child needs is secure attachments, love and laughter.

Thank you for your support of my work on this issue.

Yours sincerely,

Karen Varney

PART ONE

CASE STUDIES

Sophie

Mother of daughter, Chrissy, and son, James

Profession: Senior Psychologist

Location: Sydney, New South Wales

'No one else will ever know the strength of my love for you.
After all, you are the only one who knows the sound of my heart from inside'

- Kristen Proby

B eing a psychologist, I thought I could smooth things over by talking, which didn't work, but I know people who spent thousands of dollars in court and they are no better off than me, so it's hard to know what I could have done differently.

I grew up in Melbourne; my parents were European immigrants, and I was their second child. I have an older sister, a year and a half older than me. Before they had us, my parents made sure they were set up; operating their own business and working hard. As a child, I remember watching Mum cooking in the kitchen, and my dad doing push-ups with my sister sitting on his back. They were both very loving and affectionate, making sure they always had time for us. My sister and I were close; we even sounded the same. I remember we used to play tricks on each other; it was like I was her human toy! I used to dream of having a stud ranch so I could ride horses all day and I loved to dance. Whenever we had Greek functions, I'd always be the first one on the dance floor, especially when the Greek belly-dancing music came on, that was my favourite. I also loved breakdancing.

When I was a teenager, I wanted to be a doctor, but I wasn't sure I was smart enough! In Grade Nine, three friends and I made a pact that we would become psychologists. I was interested in science and had always had an affinity with kids. Even when I was older, if we were at a party, I always prefered to be around the kids. They were drawn to me, too. So when it came time to decide what I wanted to study, the decision was made: child and adolescent psychology. Still to this day, I am so glad my path led me there.

When I was almost seven, my parents got divorced, and I remember a lady from court asking me who I wanted to live with. I sat their silent, thinking, What a ridiculous question, I can't answer that, I want to live with both of them. Back then, the usual arrangements were the father had the kids once a fortnight for the weekend and the mum had them the rest of the time, and that's what happened with us. I coped through this by trying to make everyone laugh. On the weekends, my sister and I were with Dad, and he would take us horse riding. We started wanting to go every time. It was a long drive, but I don't think he minded, as he was always really loving and never spoke poorly about Mum. Looking back, my perception was that I just cruised through the family separation and it didn't affect me much. I'm not saying it was easy though.

Mum eventually remarried and had my sister who is ten years younger than me; that was such an exciting time. When I became a teenager, all I wanted to do was hang out with friends on the weekends, which meant Dad would sometimes miss out. He'd say, 'I only get to see you once a fortnight and you'd prefer to go out with your friends?' My sister and I learnt to value the time we had with him.

When I turned fourteen, my mum, step-dad, and two sisters decided we would move to Queensland. I guess Dad could have put his foot down, but he didn't. Looking back, that must have been hard for Dad. We made sure we never lost touch though; my sister and I would fly back and forth every school holiday.

We never rejected either of our parents or blamed either one for the breakdown. They handled it between themselves and got on with being parents. Nowadays, they are friends more than ever; it's funny how that happens.

After a few years, my also remarried but didn't have any more kids. My mum, sisters, and step-dad started talking about moving to Greece. I was in my third year of university and I had already decided I wanted to do a post-graduate degree, but after not receiving a place at the University in Queensland, I moved to Sydney to finish my studies. A year later, when my studies were over, the move to Greece became official. I was really torn; they wanted me to go, but I wasn't sure about leaving Australia and living so far away from Dad. Soon after, I met Mario, and my family started saying things like, 'You can't start a relationship now, we're moving to Greece!'

Mario attached himself to me very quickly, never wanting to be apart and constantly calling. He wouldn't even let me sleep half the time! There was a real pull towards him; he was loving, caring, and supportive, and being in Sydney I missed the closeness I had with my family. Mum flew down to Sydney to convince me to go to Greece; they even took my car and withdrew their financial support, to persuade me to go.

When Dad met Mario, he didn't think he was the person for me, but I thought he really loved me, and I had never experienced that kind of attention and affection before; it was full-on but felt right. I'd had enough of my parents' objections, so instead of listening to their advice, I said to Mario, 'Let's get married!' That year, we got engaged, I moved in with him, next door to his parents and sister, and my family moved to Greece.

Mum, Dad and his wife, still flew over for the wedding. They said, 'If you love him and this is what you want, we can't stop you.' I was ready to start my own life and make my own decisions, but I was only twenty-three and couldn't see what they saw. Mario constantly said, 'Your parents don't accept me'. Every time, I would assure him, and they did try, but as time went on, I had to hide more and more things from them because, of course, they were right.

Mario is Italian on both sides and is the cousin of a friend I had at university. The first time I met him, I didn't like him. He was charming and funny, but sleazy. He kept persevering though, and after organising for us to play in a soccer team together, he kept wanting to spend more and more time with me. I wasn't used to getting so much attention, and after a few months of it, I thought this guy really loves me! I had hoped my love would also grow, but I was always unsure and the more I got to know him, the more I thought, I'm an idiot! Everything happened so quickly; moving in, the engagement, marriage, then before I knew it, I was pregnant. I had wanted to wait until my studies and training were over, but Mario really wanted to have a family straight away. Even though it was quick, I was happy to be having a baby and when my son was born, I was still able to take him to training. It was only two days a week which meant my focus could still be on him.

Mario wasn't good at holding down a job; he didn't like working and wasn't the most enthusiastic person. He'd make friends quickly—people were drawn to him—but the friendships wouldn't last long. Every weekend, we would have new people over and I'd think, How long will these ones

6

last? Whenever he started a new job, he'd become best friends with the boss straight away, thinking he was 'in' and entitled to some sort of special treatment or instant promotion, even before others who had already been there five or ten years. He also tried every profession: driving trucks and buses; selling mobile phones; working as a security guard; and at one stage wanted to be a youth worker. We would outlay money for uniforms, training, and licenses, even when we were already struggling financially. I would say, 'Can you just stay where you are for a bit longer?' But he always had a reason, or a better idea.

It wasn't just jobs and friends he would change; we also went through sixteen cars in ten years. One time, he thought he was doing an even swap at a car yard, but for some reason, we went from having a $16,000 car to having a $3,000 bomb! He also had to have the latest phone and back then they were expensive. He would break phone contracts, then we would pay hundreds of dollars to pay out contracts to buy the latest one; he'd have one in my name, then another in his mum's. If I spoke up, even his parents would side with me! I would say, 'We need to pay this bill, maybe you should work a little more?' I would say it in a gentle way, but he'd always get upset, 'You just want to leave me, I know, you just want a divorce!' And I'd say, 'No, I'm just talking about bills!' He started bringing it up more and more, at least once a week: 'You want a divorce, you want a divorce...' and I would have to reassure him again and again.

When I was pregnant with our daughter Chrissy, Mario stayed in the same job as a security guard for a year then after we had our son, James, he really tried. I went back to work when my son was six months then again when my daughter was five months but for only twenty hours a week, so I could still be there for them. I had to work; we were really struggling, I used to do our food shopping on $60 a week; how do you feed a family of four on that? His family helped us out so much; I don't know what we would have done without them. Although everything didn't always run smoothly.

After I met Mario's family, I realised my father-in-law liked telling stories. He would say things like, 'I heard a rumour about this ... that your sister said 'this' or 'that'. Most of the time it wouldn't be true. Whenever he did this, it would cause a war and they wouldn't talk to whichever person, depending on what was said. My sister-in-law would pipe up in support of pushing the person away; she is Mario's older sister and pretty tough. Mario would sometimes be the peacemaker, stepping in to bring the family back together, 'C'mon we are family, life's too short!' He would repair the damage, then it would happen again. Sometimes the conflict would make my mother-in-law so anxious to the point of making her sick; we used to bond over it because I would try to help her through it. She was wheel-chair-bound, and my sister-in-law had to leave high school in her final year to take care of her. She never had the chance to fulfil her dreams or have a family of her own. She and I did have a lot of fun together though; we would take the kids to the show, out shopping, or to a park. We didn't want to be stuck at home; we enjoyed getting out and letting the kids have experiences. I used to laugh and say, 'I should have married you instead!'

In 2004, when our daughter was four, Mario decided to study to be a youth worker for a year. I, and his parents, were supporting him, even though they were pensioners. He struggled with the work, but I helped him as much as I could, being in my field of work. Then he'd go to school the next day pretending like it was him who knew it all!

He started staying out late; he said he was just studying with a friend called Nicole. I'd ask, 'Till five in the morning?' When he bought himself a new mobile phone, he gave me his old phone but forgot to delete his 'sent' messages (this was before smartphones) and I found all these heavy love text messages to her. I don't know what she wrote back because I could only see his messages. I rang the number; she answered and denied everything. She admitted he had sent them, but she said she didn't feel the same way. I confronted him and told him it was over, then moved into the spare room. That night, he was really emotional: hugging me, crying. I was actually afraid he might snap because I hadn't seen him that upset before. Later that night, I opened my eyes and saw him standing in the doorway watching me. I lay there frozen, pretending to be asleep.

Day by day, I hung in there until February 2008 when, out of the blue Mario said, 'I don't care about you anymore, you can leave me and I'll still let you see the kids.' Strange, because he had always firmly said, 'If you leave me you won't see the kids.' I thought, Okay, this is sounding better. Then on Valentine's Day, I bought him a gift and a card and when he read it he said, 'You don't mean that', and ripped it up in front of me. Apparently, he didn't have any money to buy me something, but a couple of days later he bought himself a new hat! A few days later, the 'You want a divorce, don't you' talk started again, and after ten years of saying, 'No' this time I said, 'Yes, I do'. He was stunned, I don't think he ever thought I'd have the balls to say it.

The next morning, when the kids were getting ready for school, Mario announced, 'Kids, your mum wants a divorce, she wants to break up.' Our daughter suggested, 'Maybe we can live one week with you and one week with Dad?' I don't think that was the response Mario wanted to hear; our son didn't say anything. Mario could be quite stern with him at times, so I think he was scared of saying the wrong thing. After I dropped them at school, it sunk in; this is it, I'm actually leaving. It was such a relief. I had held on for so long. My mind was racing. First things first: where am I going to live? I rang a few friends, and one said, 'You can stay here', so I stayed there for a week, but I was still going back to our house every day. Mario's parents offered for me to live with them, even my sister-in-law asked too! I declined the offer saying it would be too hard with Mario still living next door; it was nice they offered though. At the time, Mario was running his own courier business. He'd started it after only two weeks of working as one, and with the use of his parents' money to get it going. At the start, his parents only had forty thousand left on their mortgage and by the time Mario's business failed they were back up to a hundred and eighty. I felt I couldn't take anything more from them, so I just left and didn't ask for anything. Actually, I did leave with something—two cars both in my name—and because I knew I'd get more for mine, I sold it; but was left driving Mario's green station wagon.

The first night I had without the kids, my son called pleading with me to come home. I tried to explain, but he kept ringing and ringing. The next day, Mario put all my stuff into garbage bags then called to say, 'Come and collect your stuff'. When my son saw the bags he shouted, 'Mum! You're leaving us!' I had to quickly find somewhere for us to live. I was lucky, as within a week I found a place, only ten minutes away from the kids, in a unit on a farm next to a lovely Tuscanstyle house where the landlord lived. But while I was doing that Mario took the kids, with his parents and sister, to The Entrance, about two hours' drive north of Sydney for a three-day holiday. When I told Mario where the new place was, he said, 'Oh yeah, that's next door to this Italian family who is from the same village as us.' I thought, I don't care, I don't have anything to hide. Then he said, 'Did you know someone hung themselves in that house?' I was like, 'What?' I asked my landlord and he said it did happen but not in my house, but of course hearing that made the kids scared to stay there. Our son was already anxious and now this only made him even more so.

I became estranged from Mario's family after he told them 'I don't consider them 'family' anymore', so they all turned against me. He then told all of his relatives and our son James I was having an affair. Even though I was ready to be with someone, I wasn't sleeping with anyone. Then they said they had naked photos of me and some guy and I thought, Really? Show me them! I'd like to see them because they don't exist! Then my father-in-law said to me, 'I always thought you were a lesbian, then I thought, no, maybe a prostitute.' He told everyone I had been storing drugs at my house for a drug dealer. I said to him, 'I am still the mother of your grandchildren, maybe you should be setting the record straight, not encouraging rumours.' Then my father-in-law turned up on my doorstep, pleading for me to go back to Mario. He hugged me so tightly, it was really uncomfortable. Then the icing on the cake was while I had a friend over, and I caught my father-in-law in the front yard trying to peer in! He told Mario I had someone there and when I tried to explain who he was, it also came out what his father had been doing. That was the biggest mistake I made, telling Mario what his father had been doing. After that, my sister-in-law never spoke to me again.

Shortly after, Mum flew over from Greece to visit me and while we were in the backyard with the kids, my father-in-law confronted me, 'Did you think I wanted to get in your pants?' I was put on the spot and said, 'Umm, I don't know, you just made me feel uncomfortable.' Eight years on, Mario's sister is still angry with me. I tried everything to smooth it over, but she wouldn't listen. Mario didn't say much initially, but when he finally confronted his dad, the shit really hit the fan! His father was always the life of the party, so I think it shocked a lot of people when it came out but I had to say something; he was hiding in my front yard!

Soon after my separation from Mario, I attended a talk by Carol Boland, a Children's Court clinician who handles severe high-end cases between mothers and fathers, in court. She explained there are two different kinds of narcissists: one who is the high achiever—the golden child—with the trophy wife, the fancy car, and house; if you ever do wrong by them, you're gone! Then she explained the other type of narcissist who has a fragile, insecure ego. She said, 'If you ever want to leave a narcissist you must be very careful.' I don't want to label Mario, but psychologists understand the individual person and it's the social workers and family therapists who understand the overall relationship dynamics. We don't always see the broader perspective, but after that talk, I got it, because I lived it.

I remember, one day when we were still together, and my daughter was about seven. Mario said, 'Hey, Chrissy, we're Italian not Greek, aren't we?' and my daughter said, 'Yeah, we're Italian, not Greek!' I felt instantly invisible, realising how easily kids can be manipulated. It scared me because she would agree to anything he said. My son noticed how upset I was, so he went to the corner shop (which was next door) and bought me a little bottle of perfume, shaped like a shoe. He said, 'I've never seen my mum cry before.' I still have the bottle.

I now work with children who have parents with substance abuse history and teenagers who are using drugs and alcohol, assisting with their trauma, learning difficulties, and specific family issues. Children attach themselves to their caretaker even if they are scary or abusive; they actually cling to them even more because of the inconsistency and uncertainty.

I always thought I had a secure attachment with my kids, like my parents did with me; calm, loving, available, and positive. When we separated, Mario was really angry and upset, and it was like the children felt they needed to take care of him and thought I would probably be okay because I wasn't showing as much distress. I didn't think it was fair for

11

them to take on how I was feeling as well, so I tried to stay strong and stable for them as best I could. Three months later, Mario said, 'I was sitting in a park and I realised you were gone, and I started crying.' I think up to that point he was trying to stay angry. Then he said, 'I know some people who have separated, and they are friends; let's be like that,' and I said, 'YES! Let's be like that!' But that attitude didn't last long. I never knew what kind of mood he would be in, sometimes really friendly, then he'd be really sad then angry, he had so many mixed emotions.

For the next eight months, I tried to work things out with Mario. He agreed to sign Centrelink papers saying we would have the kids fifty/fifty, but I had no idea about all the things he and his family were saying to them behind my back. I would drop the kids at school, then when I'd pick them up, they wouldn't want to stay the night and I didn't understand why. One excuse my daughter used once was, 'I can't stay over because my auntie has been at work and I haven't seen her for a few days,' and I said, 'But I'm your mum and I haven't seen you either!' They were making the kids feel bad if they had time away from them. If they did say they wanted to be with me, Mario and his sister would put on a show, hugging them tight, saying, 'Make sure you call us if there's an emergency', like they wouldn't be safe with me. When I'd ring, they would put me on speaker and interrogate me. Once, Mario said, 'You left without the kids, therefore you didn't want them.' Loud enough for the kids to hear, of course. I said, 'I didn't leave them, I left you, I want us to be parents together.' Then I was told by the school psychologist that because I am a child psychologist, Mario thought I was going to take the kids off him, but I said, 'I would never do that; I am the one who wants us to have equal time with the kids.' It became bitter, so quickly, I thought I'd try mediation, but before you can have it, you have to have three sessions individually. Over that time, the situation deteriorated more and more, and the kids were spending less and less time with me. Mario would say, 'I really encourage the kids to see you but it's their choice, I can't force them', or 'That's what you get for leaving. It was your choice.'

In October 2008, we did do mediation. Mario attended his three sessions and I had mine, then when it came time to having our first one together, we met for coffee beforehand and he told me they were moving to The Entrance. He said that ever since the kids went on holiday there they'd wanted to go back. I couldn't believe it. At the meditation, we made a verbal agreement: I would drive up Mondays, Wednesdays, and Fridays. Mario didn't offer to meet me halfway, so I was driving two hours there to spend two hours with them, then driving two hours back home. After my third trip, the kids refused to come out. It was a weekend and I sat in my car from morning till evening refusing to leave until they came out, but they never did. My sister-in-law was yelling out, 'They don't want to see you! Go away!' I went to a soccer game to watch my son play and in front of everyone she was saying, 'You left your children!' She became really evil! I tried talking to her, reminding her of how it used to be, but she was still so angry. A month later, my daughter told me her Holy Communion was coming up. I knew it would be back in Sydney, too. I asked her how it was and told her I didn't know what day it was. Then when I asked Mario he said loudly, 'You knew when it was, you just didn't turn up. We drove past your house and saw you were home; your car was in the driveway.' He drove past to show her I was at home! From that moment on my daughter stopped speaking to me: she was eight. I thought the only thing I can do is go to court, so I got a solicitor through Legal Aid to do mediation again but through the court instead. The orders however, would still not be enforceable, but that was their advice. At the hearing, it was agreed we would have family therapy. We found a place near the kids, at Unifam in Gosford, three hours north of Sydney. I booked the appointment and was happy to drive up. I thought, It will be great to allow the kids to talk about how they are feeling and know they don't have to choose one parent over another. When I arrived the lady said, 'We weren't expecting you.' I reminded her that I had made the appointment. She said, 'Yes, but I got a call from the father saying you weren't coming. I'll get another chair.' After the first meeting, they called to say, 'We can't offer you any more sessions because it's for the children and it's a conflict of interest.' I said, 'I don't understand, I have orders from mediation saying we would have counselling?' and she said, 'No, sorry, we can't offer you more counselling.' She went on to say they could continue to see the kids but not with me. I think they went one more time then refused to go again. I realised the only

13

option I had was to pursue it further in court, but my son said, 'If you take Dad to court, we'll never see you again.' I backed off only with the promise I'd have time with the kids. Months went by and nothing happened, so I had no other choice but to take action in court. On the day of the hearing, Mario arrived in his PT Cruiser, with two Italian flags sticking out the top, you couldn't miss it. He parked it right out the front in the disabled zone. He always wanted a disabled sticker; I think he borrowed his mum's or something that day to make sure he was noticed. When I saw him I said, 'I like your flags!' and he said, 'YEAH! We're going to win!' like they were a team about to go into battle. My sister-in-law submitted her personal diary, eighty pages of rubbish about me. The magistrate opened the diary, read one paragraph and said, 'Who wrote this?' When we said it was my sister-in-law she said, 'Bring her in here. I want to see her.' When she came in, she said to her, 'I have read one paragraph and I am not reading any more because I know what's going on here. If the mother doesn't want to buy the kids an ice cream, she doesn't have to.' She went on to say in the diary that I didn't feed them and that my house stank, and they would come home smelling of my house! Apparently, I also gave them food poisoning and mosquito bites! It was ridiculous. The magistrate said, 'You are not the mother: she is (and she pointed to me) It is not your job to say this and that, it is your role to say that their mother and father love them equally, not to put the mother down; these children need to spend time with their mother.' But because all I asked for was family therapy, that's all I got. I didn't know the rules: you ask for what you want, and the magistrate decides on that alone; they can't make up what happens. My solicitor never told me. I found out when I arrived, and my lawyer said, 'Why did you only ask for therapy?' and I said, 'I don't know, I know nothing about court.' By this stage, my kids were a bit older and had a say in what they wanted. They had an independent children's lawyer, but he didn't turn up on the court day and everyone was trying to call him. He told me that, 'This is one of the worst cases of alienation and estrangement I have ever seen. The kids so vehemently don't want to see you and the father's family don't talk very highly of you.'

The therapy was approved, and I chose a place called Keeping in Contact, but Mario and the kids never turned up, so I went on my own. I learnt so much about separation. I thought, How could I be a psychologist and not know what goes on! It was crazy. The lady I saw had been working with separated families for twenty years. She advised me not to go to court, saying it was a waste of time and money; she urged me to just be gentle, consistent, and patient, consistently letting the kids know I love them, but I felt like not fighting meant I wasn't doing my duty as a mother. The more I fought and sought legal avenues, the more Mario and his family stuck their heels in. She was right.

My therapist gave me the idea of volunteering at my daughter's school. I thought I'd ring to see if I could help and they recommended I work casually in the canteen. Mario got wind of it and was quick to call my son's high school to make sure I didn't apply there too. The canteen lady at the primary school accepted me and asked if I could come in that Friday. They told me that Mario had volunteered too, and he would also be there. I laughed and said, 'Umm, okay!' But when I arrived, his sister came instead. I smiled at her and said, 'Hi!' and she just glared at me. Then Chrissy came in and she was hugging and kissing her in front of me, her auntie moving over to make sure she was in between us. My daughter was still not talking to me, but I wanted to show her I still cared and was available. I kept going every Friday; my sister-in-law never came back. My daughter would hide behind her friends as the other mums would try to help me. I'd say, 'Hi Chrissy' and smile at her, but she wouldn't say anything or smile back. Mario told her I was there to impress everyone and not there for her. When my daughter was in Grade Six, I would travel up every second Friday to volunteer, but when the year was up, Mario made sure I couldn't volunteer at her high school. I hoped Chrissy seeing me would slowly break down the walls between us, but it didn't. I still drove up at Christmas, birthdays, and Easter. I would take gifts for them; my son would come out and accept them, but my daughter never once came out. After a two-hour drive, my son would come out, answer my questions for five minutes then go back inside and I'd drive two hours back, even on Christmas Day. Sometimes on the drive back, I'd be so upset, I'd have to pull over. Once, I got so upset

15

I started to hyperventilate and couldn't breathe. I was scared that would happen again so if I felt that coming on again, I let myself have a good cry.

My therapist explained: 'Kids like to keep the peace, so wherever the tension is bubbling, they will follow what they need to, so they don't feel tension, even if it means rejecting you.'

On my son, James' birthday, my sister was in town from Greece, so I took her and her husband up to see him. When I knocked on the door he answered, then my sister-in-law opened her window and at the top of her lungs yelled out, 'Don't speak to her, she disrespected us!' My son said, 'Go back in your room!' I told him I was sorry he had to go through that on his birthday. I saw James a couple of times after that, then he refused again. I was stuck because if I reached out it would stress him out, but if I stood back and gave the kids space, I would be told, 'You don't care about them'. I couldn't win; everything I did was wrong.

The biggest hurdle has been going from such a secure attachment with the kids to complete estrangement and feeling like I have no control. I felt so lost, everything I tried didn't work. I often wonder if I should have stayed until the kids were older, so I was the one to suffer and not them, but I now know parents who have older kids and this has happened to them, too.

I have learnt that I am very resilient. No one knew at work what was going on and I didn't tell anyone from the dancing school I taught at either. I spoke to friends and made sure I stayed healthy, ate well, didn't become an alcoholic, and got sleep, because I knew if I didn't, I'd go insane. I made myself go to work every day even if I didn't feel like it.

I have very optimistic parents and family who have a very positive view on life, so I am grateful I have inherited that from them and I'm just hoping that my kids experienced enough of me to have that view, too. I know that they are loved, even though they are missing a big part of their life. Mario's family helped us a lot and the kids were always number one. You would think that would mean that they would support their relationship with me and my family, but obviously they don't see it that way.

I have some clients who have had trouble with drugs and a hard life, but they still find ways to work it out for their kids. You don't have to be highly intelligent to co-parent, it doesn't have to be hard. I feel like James and Chrissy are very isolated. I love exploring finding different interests, always learning. I wish they could do that with me. They have a niece now and I have sent photos, I hope they will come around, but my daughter is like me—she's the quiet one—which is what worries me: that she doesn't have a voice. She's a people-pleaser and wants to be a speech therapist; she was so much like me when she was little. I would lie on the couch and she would lie on my stomach; that was her spot, and we would dance together. She was such a good kid, a good learner; my son was the naughty one at school! Maybe that's why he's more outspoken and not afraid to say what he thinks. A while passed until James agreed to have dinner with me. He started crying, asking me why I left his dad. I told him we weren't suited and that we just grew apart, but I think he wanted me to say something bad so he could be angry at me again. Chrissy is more like me, always showing a calm front, so people don't see our emotions very often. I think she would hold a lot in which worries me. Chrissy's sixteen now. My son said she's really mature, hangs out with friends, and gets good grades, but doesn't dress up for boys, yet! I worry about their trust in relationships, I am sure they shut down a part of themselves, I did when my parents separated. I want my kids to know that I love them and care for them (I tell them that in cards) and that I want them in my life and there's enough love and time for everyone; they don't have to choose. If you genuinely love your kids, you don't deprive them of their other parent.

Love is infinite, you don't have to conserve it for a certain amount of people. Love is not restrictive, it doesn't make you change your identity to suit another person, it's about allowing yourself to blossom, to be the person you want to be. Overall, I think I was a great mum.

LEGAL COMMENTARY

There are signs of family violence in Mario and Sophie's relationship which became apparent from early in their relationship and strengthened following Mario and Sophie's separation. They are:

- Seeking to isolate Sophie from her family
- Emotional abuse
- Financial abuse
- Inability to retain stable employment
- Frequent conflict with family members generally.[3]

Ideally, you should seek legal advice from a specialised family lawyer before separating from your partner. This will allow you to:

- Create a safety plan (a person is most at risk of family violence in the period immediately leading to and following separation)
- Ensure you have safe accommodation which can accommodate yourself and the children
- Ensure you have the children in your care when you leave
- Ensure access to financial information from your relationship to enable advice to be obtained in relation to your settlement
- Have the primary care of the children, pending agreement of future care arrangements.

In Sophie's case, had she sought advice regarding the children immediately following separation, noting that her separation was in some ways unplanned, then a family lawyer could have tried to negotiate with Mario on her behalf, and otherwise issued urgent parenting proceedings to ensure that she was able to spend frequent time with them. Also, the signs of parental alienation could have been addressed by a family report, by way of a psychiatric assessment of Mario. Due to Sophie not seeking legal advice for almost six months, substantial damage had already occurred to her bond with the children.

Legal Commentary by Monica Blizzard Accredited Family Law Specialist (LIV)

Sally

Mum of two girls: Loren and Mandy

Profession: Chemist, BA in Science.

Location: Victoria, Australia

'My heart hurts every day as I cannot see nor speak to my children or even know how they are doing'

- Sally.

I pride myself on being honest and truthful at all times, so, working as a chemist in a male-dominated industry, sometimes my abrupt morality isn't welcomed, but people who know me often say it's one of the things they like about me. I am loud but passionate, love food, and enjoying time with friends, but most of all: I love family.

In 2012, I was the happiest woman in the world; I had a loving, healthy relationship with my partner of five years and his two children had become like my own, but the real lights of my life were my two gorgeous girls. Life was good. We travelled, shopped, ate in fancy restaurants, and on sunny days we would swim at the beach till sundown. I worked hard to give my girls the world, just as my parents did for me. I really thought we had a great relationship and that I gave them the courage and independence they needed to be themselves. I never imagined anything like this could happen to us.

My mum and dad were typical Italians, with a love and passion for food. I spent my childhood working in our family's restaurants with my brothers. Mum and I were thick as thieves; she was like a sister, a mum, and a best friend all rolled into one. She used to say, 'No sex before marriage!'. Life was all about getting married, having a family, and working hard. I was always told to be an individual and stand on my own two feet. They always supported my decisions, even if they were wrong; they were my lessons to learn. On weekends, Mum and I would go shopping, but if the sun was out, we were at the beach! We would coat our bodies in cooking oil—she said it was more effective than tanning oil—we even put it on our faces! I was really lucky, I had a great childhood.

Like most people, I had a few relationships in my twenties, then when I was twenty-eight, I met Carlos at a friend's birthday party. He was different to the others; more laid back, charming, and intelligent. He didn't care if I wanted to go out with girlfriends or that I had a career. Even when he needed a new car, I bought him one! After dating for a while, I wasn't sure If I wanted to stay together. Mum said, 'It's up to you, I can't make that decision for you.' Then one busy Saturday night, while I was working at the restaurant, bunches of flowers started arriving for me. The first bunch had a card attached saying 'Sally', the second said 'Will' the third,

'You' the fourth 'Marry' and the fifth one 'Me'. I looked up to see Carlos arrive holding the last bunch in one hand and a ring in the other. Everyone clapped and cheered as Carlos got down on one knee and asked, 'Will you marry me?' Eight months later, we were married.

On our wedding day, when I spoke to Carlos in the morning, and he was really short with me, blaming me for having a sore back after our couple's massage at the hotel the day before. When I hung up, I was shocked, I had never seen that side of him. I told my friends, but they assured me it was just pre-wedding nerves. But once we were married that kind of behaviour increased. He lost his job after we got married, which meant I was the bread-winner for the first three months. He started to compare who made more money, picking fights and saying, 'You think you're better than me.' Then out of the blue, I fell pregnant, which was a shock because I was still on the pill. I was in the middle of doing my MBA and happy to be working because my career had taken off. It all happened so quickly. Shortly after, Carlos found out his mum had cancer, so I started using that as an excuse for his behaviour. Then one day he said to me, 'If Mum dies, I'll have no family,' and I replied, 'I am your family too, and we have a baby on the way.'

Carlos never knew his father and he grew up with two older brothers who blamed him for his death. While their mum was pregnant with Carlos, they were in a car accident where their father died instantly. I guess his brothers needed someone to blame. He really attached himself to my dad, looking back I think he just craved a father figure.

After his mum passed away, Carlos insisted we move into his family home; that's when the abuse turned from verbal to physical. My cleaner and close friend (still to this day) was the only person who knew it was happening. She constantly told me to leave.

I remember the first time he hit me, I was five months pregnant and my friend, Carmel, was picking me up for a girls' weekend. When she arrived, she saw Carlos punching me in the stomach. When we left, I was crying, and I remember asking my friends what to do. They all agreed that I had to keep it quiet. They suggested that perhaps he was still upset about losing his mum and didn't know how to cope. Even though my friends didn't really like him, they'd say, 'You're MARRIED, Sally'. They were still single at that time. I know I should have told the police, but back then 'we' didn't do that and I didn't know about divorce because no one in my family had gone through one before.

I was shocked to find out I was pregnant again but excited to be giving Loren a sister. Then shortly after Mandy's arrival, my mum was diagnosed with a terminal illness. My whole world came crashing down, but I had to stay strong to make sure her last days were memorable. I asked her to write a bucket list and I spent every day trying to tick something off. The list included everything from being on television to trying a vibrator!

When Carlos and I officially filed for divorce, we just went to a 'generalist' lawyer to finalise it. I was never advised to get court orders for the girls and even though I hated Carlos for what he did, I had to put our issues aside and make sure the girls maintained a relationship with their father. We decided to increase Carlos' time with them until we had fifty/fifty access, even though he never picked them up on time or was generally interested in their activities.

I really had to work on finding myself again. I had lost my self-confidence and had put on a lot of weight from stress. I started eating well, losing weight, and working as much as I could to provide for them. I also tried to make life fun, so they had things to look forward to. They were my life.

Four years later, I met my now partner, Glen. His son and daughter grew close to Loren and Mandy and before long we became family. For Mandy's fifth birthday, we threw her a party in the park with ponies and games. Mum desperately wanted to be well enough to be there, but as soon as the party was over, she packed her suitcase and said it was time for her to go to hospital.

Two days before she passed away, Carlos begged her for forgiveness, promising he would never hurt me again. Mum said she forgave him but when he left she apparently said to Glen, 'Please don't ever let Sally go back to him, he is an evil man.'

As soon as Mum was gone, Carlos really started to play games; not returning the girls on time or answering the phone when I'd call. When I would call the police, they would ask, 'Have you got court orders?' I should have inquired more about these 'court orders', but no one ever told me how important they were or how to get them. A few years passed, then in December 2012, I heard Loren arguing with Mandy. In a rage, she said 'It's a secret between me and Dad. They are going to break up because Nerida is sick of supporting him!' I stupidly laughed because I was relieved that was all she was worried about, but then she said, 'Nerida is my best friend and I'm going to lose her, She's the only one I can talk to! You and Glen are happy, I want them to be happy too, if she leaves Dad he will be lonely.'

A month later, Loren started wanting to spend more time with her dad. The children and I were going away to America for three weeks during their summer holidays, and she said she wanted to spend quality time with him before we left, so I didn't question it. Mandy was the opposite, she even said she wanted to change her last name to mine and asked Glen if she could call him 'Dad' We said, 'No, Mandy, you already have a dad!'

At 10:00 pm, the night before our trip, Glen went to pick up the girls, but when he arrived, there was no one home. I tried to ring and text, but there was no answer. I tried calling Loren, but her phone was off.

At 11:15 pm, Carlos called me. I put him on loudspeaker so my friend Lucy could hear what he said: 'You are never going to see your kids again. I'm going to kill you. You're not going to America …'. While I was on the phone, Lucy rang the police. They told her: without court orders, no one 'owns' the kids. Defeated we hung up. Fifteen minutes later, the police called to say the girls were safe and happy, eating icecream in a park! Carlos agreed to return the girls, but only if I came into the station to sign a statutory declaration agreeing to hand over their passports when we returned, because he wanted to take them to Fiji. The policeman said, 'He was unaware you were taking the girls overseas and wants a copy of your itinerary.' I told him I booked the trip last year, and Carlos was aware of our plans. I eventually gave up agreeing to sign it. When I arrived at the police station, the officer said, 'The father has agreed to return your daughters to your house once you have signed the papers.' Finally, he warned, 'I suggest when you get back you get a court order so this doesn't happen again.' I signed the papers and went home to wait.

Two hours later, the girls arrived. Mandy ran in frantic, crying, 'Mummy, Mummy, I'm so scared!' I hugged her so tight, assuring her everything was okay. Loren walked in behind her, angry and with attitude, 'What's everyone so worried about?' I asked, 'Why didn't you answer your phone?' and she said, 'Dad told me not to talk to you. It's got nothing to do with me. Why are you putting me in the middle?' Then in a rage, she yelled, 'I don't know who to believe: YOU or DAD!'

By this time, we only had four hours before we had to get up, so I did my best to settle them then tucked them into bed. When I finally got to bed, Glen said, 'I think you should check on Mandy again, she told me she's really scared because when they were in the car, Nerida and Carlos said, 'As soon as we get home they're going to take us away from you and Mum'. I think you should talk to her again.'

When I went back into Mandy's room, she was still wide awake, in tears. I assured her that 'they' can't take her and Loren away and that Daddy probably just said those things in the heat of the moment. I gave her countless kisses, and said, 'How exciting! We're going OVERSEAS! We need to get some sleep, so we can get up early and get ready!'

The next morning, we didn't talk about the night before. My close friend Lucy and I were taking them on the trip of a lifetime, and I wanted them to enjoy every minute. We landed in New York first, where we would stay for two weeks. It was cold, but we had such a great time; we went ice skating and to The Big Toy Shop in Central Park. We saw shows on Broadway, went shopping and ate lots of pizza! I think Mandy's highlight was buying an American doll, which was on the top of her list! After New York, we flew to Los Angeles, where we joined all our dancing friends from home: mums and daughters. Mandy was dancing at Disneyland, so we had a whole week there. Our trip was exactly how we had imagined it; we all had a ball. While we were away, I asked the girls several times if they wanted to call their dad and they both said, 'No!' Mandy even went as far as saying, 'If I never see my dad again, I'll be okay! He's really strict and yells at us.'

I said, 'You still need to see your dad, he is part of your life.' She went on to tell Lucy she was worried she won't be able to take her American doll to her dad's house, because if she is naughty or says something wrong, he will break it. 'That's what he does to anything Mum has bought me, he 'hurts' it.'

When we originally booked the trip, Loren asked if she could fly back earlier because she didn't want to miss out on the start of the school year. So I organised for her to travel back with some of our dancing friends. I asked if she wanted her dad to pick her up and she said 'No, I want Glen to'.

In the car, Glen asked her what she wanted to do and she said: 'Can I go to Dad's tomorrow? I want to see Nana Lill (Glen's mum), Jo, and Daniel (Glen's kids).' She sent her dad a text saying, I'll see you tomorrow then she spent the rest of the night describing every detail of their trip and how much fun they had: 'Mum even danced with buskers in the street!'

The next morning, Glen dropped Loren at her dad's so she could pick up her things for school. When she came back out, she said 'Don't worry Glen, Dad will take me to school. See you Sunday night' and kissed him goodbye.

It took three years to piece together what happened over the next few days, from reports and documents subpoenaed for court. I was completely oblivious to what Carlos was doing and saying. We were all completely unaware our lives were about to change forever.

Thursday

8:00 am: Glen drops Loren at her dad's house and tells him he will take her to school. Instead, Loren spends the next three-and-a-half hours at her dad's. I still, to this day, don't know what happened during this time.

11:30 am: Loren arrives at school and goes straight to the school principal, saying she would like to make some complaints about her mother; that I have been physically and verbally abusing her. The principal rings Carlos for an explanation. He said he had noticed bruises before, but thought they might have been from school sport. He said he knew I could get angry easily but didn't know how volatile it had become. They decided that Carlos should take Loren to the police and officially report the abuse to the Department of Health and Human Services (DHHS).

Friday

Mandy, Lucy, and I arrive home. Mandy asks if she can catch up with her friends first before going to her dad's. She was excited to tell them all about her trip and to give them the presents she had bought. I sent Carlos a text saying, I'll drop Mandy off at 5:30 pm, so she can see her friends after school. I keep to my word and that afternoon drop Mandy back to her dad's.

Sunday

When I picked the girls up, Loren was in a panic because she had so much homework to do, her dad would never let her do it at his place. Other than that, it seemed as though we were back to our old routine.

Wednesday

It was a public holiday the following day so Glen's daughter, Jo (Loren's best friend), came around for a sleepover. They stayed up all night watching their favourite show Nikita; we bought the series on DVD while we were away. They loved it so much!

That day, I also had a call from the school telling me Loren's school fees were outstanding. Carlos and I had an agreement that I would pay Mandy's fees and he'd pay Loren's. Mandy's were up to date, but Loren's hadn't been paid since February 2012. When we agreed, I made sure Carlos had all the details on how to pay and notified the school about the changes, but Carlos told them he didn't have the details and couldn't afford it.

Thursday

Carlos asked to pick up the girls early that morning, but they wanted to make pancakes for breakfast, so Glen sent him a text saying, Can the girls have another few hours? At 12:00 pm, Carlos sent a text to Loren saying he was out the front, which was strange because he never picked them up, we always dropped them off to his house. As usual, Loren kissed me, Glen, and Jo goodbye saying, 'Love you, love you Mum, miss you already.'

Mandy, on the other hand, clung on to me pleading, 'Please, Mummy, I don't want to go, please don't make me go, I want to stay here.' I said, 'No, Mandy, you have to spend time with your dad.' She started begging, saying, 'PLEASE!', I assured her it was okay and that she would see us again on Sunday. I almost had to push her out the door, she was in such a panic. She finally walked away saying, 'Mummy, I love you! Mummy, I love you!' I called out, 'I love you, too.' Little did I know, she was upset because she knew Carlos was taking them straight to the police station.

In the statement, the girls said things like: 'My mum calls me 'Scatterbrain''. That was the nickname their dad used to call them. If you looked at the reports and replaced ''mum' with 'dad', it's exactly what their dad had done and said—not me. That night, I got a call from the school principal asking if we could have a meeting tomorrow at 5:00 pm. I asked, 'What it was regarding?' presuming it was about the school fees. She wouldn't elaborate over the phone. 'We would like you to come in at 5:00 pm tomorrow, we can discuss the details then.'

Friday

I received a text message at 3.30 pm, saying, Please call the Faulkner Police. I thought it was to follow-up from what happened the night before our trip, but then I was directed to their 'SOCIT' unit.I was so confused, I said, 'What's going on?' and the officer said, 'We are the Sexual Offences and Child Investigative Team' and I said 'What is this about?' She said, 'You need to come into the police station, we are putting an intervention on you because you have been physically and verbally abusing your children. You need to appear in the Magistrates Court on Monday.' I couldn't believe what I was hearing. I told her, 'I've never done anything. We've just come home from a holiday together. I don't know what you're talking about?' I tried to explain what Carlos had done before we left, and she said, 'That's irrelevant! Your daughters have made complaints.' Then when they said I wasn't to contact the girls, the penny dropped with the school. I rang a close friend, Dee, to see if she could come with me to the meeting. The principal told us she had reported me to the Department of Health and Human Services (DHHS) and had advised Carlos to take the girls to the police station. I said, 'I haven't been abusing my children!' and she said, 'Children

27

don't lie!' I was so upset and confused. I told her I couldn't continue the conversation and left. I didn't understand why she would believe this. I was really involved with the school—the families and teachers—and very active within the school community. Nothing made sense. I went back to the police station, but no one bothered to ask me for a statement, they just gave me paperwork for the court hearing: Monday at 10:00 am.

Saturday

I didn't have a lawyer, so I spent all day ringing around to find one. Glen contacted a friend who was a barrister. He said if I paid him $1,800 he would represent me on Monday. I had to find a lawyer too. I didn't know what a lawyer did in the Magistrates Court; I had no idea what the process was. One finally called me back Monday morning, but she was only a 'generalist', I didn't know what that meant. Later, I found out she's like a 'GP' of lawyers: one who covers a wide variety of law. I also had to ask my new boss if I could have more time off. I had already had time off to go overseas, now I had to tell her I needed more time off to go to court.

Sunday

Today I would usually pick up the girls, but the police gave Carlos permission to keep them until we went to court.

Monday

Glen and Lucy came into court with me. I had to quickly brief my barrister. When we walked past Carlos, he stuck his foot out and kicked Glen in the shin! Lucy said, 'Did you see that?' Everyone overlooked it, so the four of us kept walking.

Inside, I was a nervous wreck; ropable, sobbing, almost like I was in a dream. Carlos was representing himself and the police were representing the children. I pleaded not guilty. The judge said to the police officer:

'Have there been any previous incidences?'

'No'

'Have there been any previous reports?'

'No'

'Was the mother ever charged?'

'No'

'Was the mother interviewed?'

'No'

They had no evidence and no history of abuse.

That morning, Carlos called DHHS and said, 'I am in court and the mother hasn't turned up. I am supposed to return our kids back to her, but I am scared for their lives!' I didn't know he made that call until a year later when I read the subpoenaed paperwork.

The judge said, 'The children will go back to their normal regime, with the mother having the understanding that she is not to verbally or physically abuse the children.' The case was then adjourned until the 30th of May (six weeks later) to decide if we go to trial.

I asked my barrister to ask Carlos when I could pick up the girls. He said to tell me to send him a text message at 2:00 pm to arrange it. At 2:00 pm, I sent him a text and he wrote back, No, I am not returning the girls to you unless you sign a piece of paper saying you will never abuse them again. I rang my lawyer for advice and she said, 'Tell him that if he doesn't return them immediately and follow the court orders, you will file for a recovery order and he will have to cover the costs.' I asked her, 'How do I know if the girls are okay?' and she said, 'You can do a welfare check or ask some close friends, who your girls trust and know Carlos, to go to the house and check on them.' I asked Dee and Myer, two of my close friends, who had known the girls since birth, and Carlos since we were married, if they would go. When they arrived, Carlos refused to let them in. They told me they could hear the girls inside, but when they called out there was no reply. Carlos called the police to report that there were two unknown women at his door trying to get in. Although he still managed to give them their names and details because the police called them to tell them to leave.

The next day, Carlos called Loren and Mandy's school teachers to say they needed to stay home because he feared I might kidnap them from school.

I spent the whole day writing an affidavit with a new barrister. If breaches aren't seen to be urgent, recovery orders can sometimes take months to be heard. I was advised to rehash every detail of mine and Carlos' past to highlight the urgency. The barrister managed to secure a court date within two weeks. For those two weeks I was climbing the walls; I couldn't eat, sleep, or work. Glen made sure someone was with me constantly. I was a mess.

May 8 2013 – Recovery Order, Federal Australian Family Court.

The judge said, 'There is something psychologically wrong with the father.' Then she looked at me and said, 'Why did you give him so much time with the children? You gave him too much access.' I couldn't win. I get told off for not giving him enough time and now scolded for giving him too much! She went on to say, 'I find this hard to comprehend, there have not been any previous incidences, the mother has never been charged, she takes her children overseas for three weeks, it seems to me this father is jealous they had a wonderful holiday without him.'

The final decision was to do an '11F' by June 11th (Family Law Act 1975 - Sect 11F; A court may order parties to attend, or arrange for the child to attend, appointments with a family consultant) The girls were to be returned IMMEDIATELY to my care and Carlos be restricted to only seeing them once a fortnight and for one weekend. He started to panic, saying he must see the girls before they come back to me. The school teachers were to notify Loren and Mandy of the new arrangements and neither of us were to discuss any of the day's events with them.

The judge also said that she was unable to comment on what was happening in the Magistrates Court, as it was a separate case. I was still due in Magistrates Court on May 30th for the intervention order Carlos had tried to put on me.

The next day, I picked up Mandy from school (Loren was at school camp). I threw my arms around her and hugged her so tight then asked, 'What would you like to do, we can do anything you like?' She said she wanted to see Nana Lill, Jo and Daniel, so we drove to their house; they were all so excited to see her. She chatted all night about our overseas trip and, like old times, we had a lovely family dinner. That night, Mandy asked if she could sleep with me because she said she was too scared to be alone.

When I picked up Loren from school, she was standing next to her teacher, on the phone to her dad. As I walked up, they were both glaring at me. I knew something wasn't right so I asked, 'What's wrong?' and the teacher said, 'We know you've bashed your children!' I was so shocked, I said, 'No, I haven't!' She said, 'Children don't lie and if you touch her again, we'll be on to you!' I found out later (through the subpoenaed documents) that while Loren was at camp, she stood up in front of everyone to announce: 'I'd like to share with everyone that my mum has been bashing me and verbally abusing me!'

Loren refused to hug me, she wouldn't even look at me. She just said, 'I don't want to be with you, I want to be with my dad!' I took a deep breath and got into the car. Trying to make the conversation positive, I asked, 'What do you feel like for dinner? Your choice', and she said our local Greek restaurant. So, Loren, Mandy, and I met Lucy at the restaurant. When we went to order, Loren said, 'We don't want to share with you. Mandy and I will order our own food!' I said, 'Okay, if that's what you'd like to do, we won't touch your food.'

The next morning, Loren asked to go to her dad's because she had left some things at his house. I wasn't allowed to discuss the court's arrangements with her, so I didn't argue. We drove her to her dad's and waited out the front for twenty minutes. When she finally came out, she was even more angry than before. They weren't due to see Carlos for another week.

On Saturday, Loren played soccer. Daniel (Glen's son) later told me, 'Loren's dad was at the game, I saw him pointing and talking right up in her face.' A few days later, before school, Loren and I had an argument because she refused to have a shower. Then in her room, I heard her talking in a panic to someone, 'Miss Harris, Miss Harris, she's screaming at me, she's coming into my room, she's going to hit me.' I took the phone off her and said, 'Hello, who is this?' and they said, 'I heard how you were talking to her!' I said, 'I'm not even touching her and who gave you permission to speak to my daughter?' She replied, 'DHHS.' We agreed to meet at school the next day to discuss this further.

I asked Glen to come with me in case I needed a witness. Loren's teacher said, 'I heard the way you were speaking to Loren.' Then, in unison, my daughters started swaying back and forth saying, 'We're really scared of her, we're really scared of her!' It was like they were hypnotised. Glen stepped in and said, 'I was there and they were arguing, but Sally didn't touch her.' Then the teacher said, 'Well, I don't scream at my children.' I later called DHHS to ask if they ever give a teacher permission to speak to a child and they said, 'No, we would never do that.' They also advised me to make sure I was never alone with the girls; that way they couldn't make any new allegations.

A few days later, I found out I had to have an operation to remove some cancerous spots on my ovaries. I told Glen I didn't want Loren and Mandy to know, but he ended up needing to tell them where I was.

While I was in hospital, the girls stayed at our friend Dee's house; they would have sleepovers there a lot because Dee's daughter, Lisa, and Mandy were best friends. While they were there, Loren told Dee she thought I was lying about being sick for sympathy. Mandy opened up to Dee, saying, 'That night you came to Dad's house, my dad and Nerida said I couldn't speak to you, but I could hear you outside and I was so scared.' Loren kept talking over her saying, 'Don't speak. Don't speak!' When I got home, Mandy hugged me tightly and said 'Mummy, I was so worried, are you okay?' but Loren had no empathy.

May 30 2013 – Magistrates Court: the hearing to address Carlos's intervention order.

The judge said: 'I can't believe you have brought this case to me. If you think I am going to allow a father, who is clearly jealous that the mother supports his children financially, and takes them on trips to America, that is ridiculous. If I allow this to go on in this court, I am allowing every other father to turn up to a police station to make allegations against a mother when they are clearly not true.' The case was dismissed immediately. Carlos was furious!

I now know from subpoenaed documents that after that appearance in court, Carlos' calls to the DHHS became frequent. At no time did they ever investigate any of his claims.

May 30 – June 6

During this time, the girls were with me. Then before school pick up, I received a call from a woman from DHHS telling me, 'Don't bother picking up Loren and Mandy from school, we will see you back in Children's Court tomorrow.' I said, 'But we have a court date in the Family Court on the 11th of June for an 11F?' and she said, 'No, the Children's Court overrides that court.' Note: State/Government Court overrides Federal Family Court. She went on to say, 'You are the most violent mother we have ever met', and I said, 'But we have never met? No one at the department has ever interviewed me.' She cut me off to tell me to come in and collect my subpoenaed documents. My lawyer called her back on my behalf, saying, 'You will courier the documents to me, I am representing Sally!' The next day, I was back in the Children's Court with another judge who said that the children appeared to be in grave danger, due to the amount of complaints the DHHS have had, and that I am a 'very violent women.' They granted Carlos' application for a supervision order and told me I was not to go near the children; if I did, I would go to jail. There was no acknowledgment of any of our previous appearances in either courts and still no evidence of abuse; DHHS never interviewed me, nor any of my family or friends, or any of the girls' relatives or close friends. There wasn't even one query into any of Carlos' or the girls' allegations, which definitely wasn't due to any of us not being open to it; if anything, we all welcomed it. It was like they had their villain and that was that, I was guilty.

A few weeks later, back in the Children's Court, my barrister was able to convince the court to do a clinical psychological report. He said to me, 'I need to get your case out of the Children's Court, if I can't you'll be stuck there for years!'

For a clinical psychological report to be processed through the Children's Court, it can sometimes take up to three months. So, my barrister asked if I was willing to pay for a private forensic psychologist to conduct the court report, as it would be done quicker, be more professional, and would be our best chance of exposing what had happened. He requested that Carlos and the department pay half, but of course, they said 'No'. It sounded like the only thing I could do. My barrister told the court I would pay for it. It cost me $8,800. Both Carlos and I were allowed to nominate an unlimited number of friends or family to be interviewed. The psychologist interviewed Carlos, Nerida, Glen, who had been my partner for six years, his fourteen-year-old daughter, Jo, and sixteen-year-old son, Daniel. Everyone, individually. Then they interviewed me, both the girls, then the girls and me together, then Carlos and the girls. Carlos didn't put any of his friends or family forward. He only put forward the girls' school teachers. The list I gave them was a mile long with additional friends and family to call or interview. I had absolutely nothing to hide and this was my chance to prove my innocence. No one's story matched the allegations Carlos or the girls had made.

On August 1st, Carlos took the girls to see a general practitioner; this doctor then sent a report to DHHS saying the children had been suffering severe headaches from all beatings I had been giving them. When I read this in the subpoenaed documents, I made an appointment with this doctor. I refreshed his memory on who the girls were and together we referred to his notes. I said, 'Did you ask my children how long it had been since they had seen me?' and he said 'No, I only report what the children tell me.' I said, 'Do you know I haven't seen my children since the 7th of June? Do you think it's possible for a child to have a headache from the 6th of June to the 3rd of August?' He was speechless; he knew he had done the wrong thing. I reported him to the medical board but the allegations still stuck.

August 5

The forensic psychologist's report was submitted back into court for review. The report said, 'My findings are that this situation is parental alienation.' She recommended that the children be spilt up immediately, that if they continued to stay together, Loren would 'highly influence Mandy to

34

believe things that weren't true.' She called it 'triangulation'; she could see that Loren had been heavily manipulated by her father. DHHS rebutted, saying it was a biased report because I funded it and that it was clear the psychologist wrote what she did because I paid her to. This was their angle in attempting to get the report taken off the record. The judge defended the highly qualified psychologist's findings, saying, 'Clearly, from this report, there are other things going on within this family, therefore this case is best suited to be handled in Family Court.'

The date for Family Court was set almost immediately. I had heard DHHS were invincible; have a never-to-expire 'get-out-of-jail-free card' and unlimited tax-payers' money to make sure parents were brought to justice, or in this case, prove I was wrong. They were not happy, and boy did it show. At the hearing, they had three government DHHS barristers and Carlos' lawyer— who was also a barrister—all against my lone barrister: one against four. We were only in there for an hour. DHHS quoted every single detail, repeatedly saying, 'This is not within your jurisdiction.' They had their reference book opened, quoting specific DHHS jurisdiction. One after the other, they listed why their laws override Federal Family Court, telling the judge she didn't have the right to decide the outcome, only they did. One of them said, 'We don't believe this court has the right jurisdiction for this case because she is a violent mother and we need to protect the children from her.' All these claims but still no evidence of abuse.

My barrister was confident that because there was no evidence, the Federal Court could override the existing rulings, however, they won. The judge said, 'I am sorry, this case is out of my jurisdiction and needs to go back to Children's Court.' To me, she said, 'I hope you see your children before Christmas.' Lucy and I were bawling. When we left, my barrister said, 'I don't know why, but the DHHS really hates you.'

It didn't take long until we were back in the Children's Court to do another psychological assessment, this time with a Children's Court clinician of the DHHS' choosing. Every time we appeared in court, I paid my barrister $3,200. I was also paying my lawyer $400 an hour to write up all the paperwork and communicate the information. Carlos went through DHHS, so he didn't have to pay a cent; every one of his appearances was completely government funded. The DHHS-appointed 'free' court clinician submitted his report to the court. He said that the previous forensic psychologist didn't know what she was talking about and our situation is not parental alienation. He believed the story that he had heard from the children; he thought that I had committed some form of violent act on the children, but he couldn't specify exactly what. He surmised, that by the way the children presented themselves, something must have happened, and it is something that I would not disclose. This clinician didn't interview me with my children. He made the assessment with Carlos and the children, and with me on my own. He didn't bother to interview me with my children. He verified what the DHHS workers wanted, which matched what they said in court, so they were happy with his findings.

In the Children's Court, you have a different judge every time and I have been told that due to the volume of cases and paperwork they generally side with the DHHS. Whereas in Federal Family Court you have the same judge for the whole case so they can assess the situation thoroughly.

October 13 2013 – Children's Court: This report took four months to process. To date, I had spent $92,000 in legal fees.

The judge found, 'The children were highly distressed and that they were to remain in the care of the father and a process of reunification was needed with the mother and children.' It was also recommended that the DHHS 'try to repair their relationship with the mother, because it is clear that the way they had treated her was unfair.'

It was 'D' Day. My options were: go to trial or sign off on the supervision order for twelve months, which would place the girls solely in Carlos' care. By me signing, I was admitting to abusing my children. It didn't matter that there was no evidence. I was told if I signed it, I would start the reunification process and see my children and that DHHS would solve the problems we had.

The DHHS put forward the maximum amount of days they could for a trial (55) then I was quoted over $250,000 in legal costs. My lawyer told me, 'Even if you go to trial, it doesn't mean you're going to get your kids back.' My barrister, who had supported me and successfully won all of our Federal Court hearings said he couldn't represent me any further and advised I find a barrister who understood the Children's Court process better. The new barrister said: 'Don't you think this is better (the agreement)—you're going to see your children, you're going to get reunification, how exciting, this is going to be great for you. Why would you want to go to trial and torment your kids?' I asked if I could have some dates for reunification and for the court orders to be tighter, but they just kept saying, 'I'm sorry, this is all we can do.' I was at a crossroad; I had spent all my money; I was gutted. It took me three hours to sign the document, even though I didn't want to; I was delirious, vomiting into a bag a friend was holding open for me. There were three other witnesses who can verify this was the advice I was given: if I want to see my children, I need to sign the supervision order. No one could be bothered finding out the truth; they just wanted to get rid of me and had decided I was guilty without any evidence or allowing me to prove my innocence. After hours of confusion and a bucket of tears, I was bullied into signing the agreement.

As soon as I signed it, the DHHS transferred my case to a new caseworker and nothing was put in place. I was told The Bouverie Centre (a government family counselling service) were going to conduct the reunification, but when I called, they said, 'No, you aren't part of the therapy, we are only involving the family.' I tried to tell her that I was the mother and I had court orders and they said, 'Sorry, we aren't aware of any of that.' Three months later, I still hadn't heard from the DHHS or started the reunification process. My only choice was to subpoena the Department back to the Children's Court to try and get some answers.

January 2014 – Seven months since I had seen my children.

When the day arrived to go back to the Children's Court, a male colleague from work offered to join me for support. While we were waiting in the foyer, a DHHS representative approached me and firmly said, 'Can you step outside, please? We have a subpoena which overrides your subpoena, but we can't legally hand it to you while we are inside the building. So, will you please step outside?' I refused. This lady was so abrasive my work colleague stepped in and said, 'Excuse me! Stop bullying her!' She turned to him and said, 'Who are you? Sally's lawyer?' and he said 'No, but you shouldn't be speaking to her like that.' She said, 'Step aside!' I was shaking and so emotional, but I had to stand my ground, everyone in the foyer was staring at me as she called the police over and they surrounded me like I was a criminal. The DHHS representative then asked me again, in front of the police, to step outside, and I said, 'No, I want to see my children and start the reunification process, as I was promised.' She disappeared to get a judge to sign their subpoena instead. While she was gone, I went to the Legal Aid counter to ask for advice and they said, 'No, we can't help you, because you earn too much money.' The foyer is completely open, so everyone could hear me and see my distress. A lady nearby was listening; she said she was a legal aid lawyer and asked what the problem was. I explained to her about the supervision order they made me sign and that the DHHS hadn't started the therapy they promised. She said, 'If DHHS get a subpoena on you, you won't be able to present the evidence you have to the court.' Their subpoena was charging me for breaching Section 121 of the Family Law Act: Restriction on publication of court proceedings. After what had happened and how I was treated, I wanted the world to know, so I wrote to politicians and to The Age and Herald Sun newspapers. DHHS had copies of them all. Not at any stage did my lawyer tell me not to send letters or that I could be in trouble for doing so.

The legal aid lawyer, Jan, offered me fifteen minutes of her time so she could look over my paperwork. When she read the terms of the supervision order, she said, 'Why did you sign this? You have admitted you are guilty. You should have gone to trial.' I said, 'But they said that it would cost me 200k plus', and she said, 'It doesn't matter if you're not guilty; unfortunately, the department will get their way, but from what I can see, you haven't done anything because there's no evidence.' That's when I knew I had been played, the department and my legal representation had no intention of doing the reunification process, they just wanted to get rid of me.

Our next hearing wasn't scheduled until October 2014, a year later, so if I hadn't subpoenaed them back to court, Carlos and the DHHS were happy for me to not see my children for a whole year. Jan agreed to come into court with me and see what she could do. In the courtroom, we had a new judge, who didn't know anything about the case, Carlos, who was

38

self-representing, the DHHS with their barrister, the children's lawyers, and me with my new lawyer I had found in the foyer. I wasn't allowed to speak. Carlos stood up and said, 'We are here today because we want to charge the mother.' He held up the letters I had written. He must have obtained copies from the DHHS, as I hadn't copied him on any of the emails. The judge said, 'I can't charge the mother; if you seriously think this is a chargeable offence you need to go to the police and charge her.' Jan stood up and said, 'I'm just briefing the mother on this; I'm not her lawyer, but based on what I have read we will be presenting this case in County Court.' When we walked out, I said to Jan, 'What's County Court?' She said, 'County Court is the only court that can override a Children's Court decision. Make an appointment with my office and come and see me.'

May 2014 – County Court, Pre-trial hearing

I was on the stand. I didn't know I was going to be put on the stand. The DHHS barrister cross-examined me. She said, 'When you signed the supervision order you had a barrister and lawyer present and they were both giving you legal advice. Are you telling me they didn't inform you of your legal rights?' I said, 'Yes, they explained the two options: to sign the order or have a fifty-five-day trial. You were there, you have all that paperwork, don't you?'

Apparently, after I signed the supervision order (October 2013) I had thirty days to file for County Court and I should have received the paperwork to do so. I never received any such paperwork, nor did my lawyer advise me that disputing the order in County Court was an option. When we went back in to hear the pre-trial dates, the DHHS said they weren't ready to go to trial, so the judge told us to come back another day to secure the dates. The trial was booked for November 2014, but when we went back to secure the dates, we found out they were meant to book a ten-day trial and had only booked for five. The trial was rescheduled for February 2015.

October 2014 – Children's Court

The twelve-month supervision order had ended, but because we were now going to County Court, the DHHS asked to extend the supervision order for another twelve months because there had been no reunification. Their request was approved.

For the County Court trial, Jan quoted me $35,000, then in December 2014, I asked if we were going to start sending out subpoenas, because I knew the DHHS had already. She agreed, but I heard nothing until January 2015 (one month before the trial) when she called to say, 'I've been thinking over the holidays and if you want me to represent you I will now need $100,000 but if you have $100,000 to spend you are wasting your time going to County Court; the department is planning to pull out their 'big guns' for your case.' Also, the barrister she had appointed (who also did work for the DHHS) had decided at the last minute not take on my case. I asked if she thought the DHHS might have bullied her, but she just reiterated, 'The barrister I have briefed no longer wants to take on your case, so we need to find another one.' She went on to say she thought I would probably lose the case and that the department will keep going until I run out of money. She said, 'This case won't get your kids back and 'they' will never let you win.'

I was hysterical by this stage. She tried to calm me down by saying she had a new plan. 'I want to try something different. Let's go back to the Children's Court and get another court report written by Dr Stuartson. I will subpoena everyone back into the Children's Court, but I won't tell them what it's about, then when we get there, we can present what we want to do.' Jan cancelled the County Court trial and subpoenaed the department back to the Children's Court where the request for a third psychological assessment by Dr Sturartson was granted.

June 2015

For the first time in two years, in front of Dr Stuartson and the head court clinician Dr Burrows, I saw my daughters. We had exchange students staying with us, so I brought them with me because they knew my story and said, 'But, you're a great mother, we want to come in and tell them how fantastic you are.' Glen's ex-wife, Alice, came along and Glen's daughter, Jo, too.

Dr Stuartson said, 'The girls can speak to you, but you aren't allowed to speak to them, do you understand? You are not allowed to cry, just smile.' I sat in silence, waiting, trying not to cry. When the girls walked in, Loren looked at me and said, 'Wipe that smile off your face, I know it's a fake. Dr Stuartson said, 'No Loren, your mother is smiling because she's happy to see you.' Loren said, 'No, it's a false smile.' When Mandy walked in, she had her head down and wouldn't look at me. Loren started yelling: 'I don't love you, get out of our lives, we don't want to see you anymore, don't you get it? We will only see you if you tell the courts what you've done ...' I had to sit there and not say anything, not even 'I love you' or 'I'm sorry for your pain'. Nothing. Mandy sat in silence. Dr Stuartson said, 'Look, your mum has brought in a photo of your dog!' Loren said, 'We don't have a dog, she's making that up.' Then Mandy said, 'Can I look at the photo?' She took the photo of their dog 'Woofy' and just stared at it. That was my ten minutes with my girls.

July 2015 – Children's Court

Dr Stuartson's recommendations were that the reunification process should be undertaken with the Children's Court clinician, and the sessions need to be conducted for three months. Then, after three months, we were to come back to court in October. At no time did the head court clinician or the appointed clinician show any empathy towards me. They kept saying, 'Just admit you've done something'. The two head clinicians from The Bouverie Centre sat in a room with me saying, 'Why don't you just admit you've done it, all you need to do is tell the truth, Sally, and this will all go away.' Apparently, 'Children do not LIE, so you must be lying?' These people were students training at La Trobe University. The first session, I met the girls individually and it was disastrous. I met Loren first and she basically she said she didn't want to see me, and that her dad had told her about all the things I had apparently done to him when we were married. She screamed at me, 'I don't love you, you only represent fifty per cent of my chromosomes, you're nothing to me.' I said 'Loren, I love you, I am sorry you feel like that, I can't admit to something I haven't done.' I got up to leave and she screamed, 'YOU SIT DOWN, I'M NOT FINISHED WITH YOU!' She was so loud that Glen, who was sitting down the hall, heard her.

41

I said, 'I love you, goodbye' and walked out. I was sobbing uncontrollably so the clinician said, 'Maybe you shouldn't see Mandy in this state?' and I said, 'No I'll be fine, I want to see her.' We walked into another room and waited. Mandy walked in like a programmed robot: 'You represent fifty per cent of my chromosomes, get out of my life.' I couldn't help but laugh a little, it was exactly the same mantra as Loren's, like a script they had to follow. Mandy loves shoes, so I said, 'Hey Mandy, do you like my shoes?' and for a moment I broke the 'script' and she said, 'Why did you tell all the girls at school not to talk to me? It's your fault they don't talk to me.' I said to the clinician, 'Could you please tell Mandy about the letter their dad gave the school?' Mandy said, 'My dad wouldn't have told my friends to not to talk to me, it's got nothing to do with my DAD!' The clinician said, 'No, Mandy, it has to do with court proceedings.' I said, 'Why are you lying to her, tell her the truth!'

In May 2013, Carlos' lawyer wrote a letter to me and the school saying that if the daughters of my close friends, specifically Dee's daughters attempt to talk to Loren or Mandy at school, he would put an intervention order on them. The clinician didn't believe me. I had the letter as proof and still Mandy said, 'No, Dad said you wrote the letter!' Then she started to panic saying, 'I'm really scared, I'm scared of my mum, get me out of here.' Before she walked out the clinician asked, 'Mandy, would you like to see your mum again?' and she said 'Yes, I would like to see my mum again, but get me out of here!' For a moment, I had a glimpse of the old Mandy again.

The next session was postponed for two weeks because Carlos claimed Mandy wasn't available. I said to the clinician, 'That's too long to wait, he will brainwash her,' and she said, 'No, Nerida, Loren, and Carlos all support this decision too.' I asked if I could bring Woofy, the girls' dog, in and she agreed that was a great idea. Two weeks later, I excitedly arrived with Woofy. Mandy loved him so much, but when I arrived, they said, 'Sorry, Sally, I have some bad news. Mandy's lawyer rang yesterday to say Mandy didn't want to come. Carlos said he tried everything to get Mandy to agree to the visit, but it was Mandy's wishes not to and he can't force her.' I was hyperventilating, crying so loud, Glen consoling me and Woofy on a lead when the head clinician yelled: 'STOP THAT CRYING, WHO DO YOU THINK YOU ARE?

If you compare the DHHS reports to the girls' school reports, they don't correlate. In August 2015, the DHHS report says: 'The children are really happy with their dad'. But when you compare it to the report from their school, it says: 'They are scared of their dad; he throws things at them, screams, and hits them'. All this information is on the subpoenaed documents I received in August 2016. Three years after my girls were taken.

October 2015 – Children's Court

The court clinician presented her report. She suggested we put the children aside, and start reunification with the parents. She said, 'The real issue is the mum and dad; the children can't be tormented anymore.' She asked the DHHS to think of a process. Their recommendation was to have all the court clinicians together to have a meeting in November 2015, including: my psychologist, the school psychologist, the lady who was looking after Carlos and the girls at Bouverie, the DHHS representative and two members from the Pops Parenting Program/Catholic Care; there were only two specialists who were supporting me invited. They decided that therapy needed to be given to the mother and the father. Nothing was put in place. I continued to see my psychologist, but Carlos did nothing. Their decision wasn't court ordered, so it didn't need to be enforced. The school psychologist wrote in her notes: 'Carlos has the power to stop this process.' By this stage, our case had been in the Children's Court for over two-and-a-half years, and by law cases can only remain in the Children's Court for up to two years, so in January 2016, when we went back into the Children's Court the judge said, 'This case can no longer stay in this court, it has to move on, it's way beyond its shelf life!'

The case was moved back into Family Court, however, DHHS still followed us and was still involved in the process. In March 2016, the DHHS agreed they would step out only if I agreed to their terms and conditions: I was to have no contact with the children at all. I had to agree to that for

43

them to leave the court case. My barrister (the good one from the start!) said that for the sake of getting 'them' out, just agree to the terms.

My barrister recommended that we go to Family Court, so we had to wait for a date. He believed we would get a quicker trial date than in Federal Court. It was also suggested another lead psychologist be involved, to whom I had to pay $6,800 upfront and $420 an hour for her services. She was appointed to figure out our family dynamics, and undertake the reunification using a rare treatment called 'paradox intervention theory', which is a form of reverse psychology. I started with her in July 2016 and completed two sessions in eight weeks. Unfortunately, this therapist too wasn't on my side.

October 2016

The Family Court judge (the one I originally had three years prior) was shocked to hear I hadn't seen my children for three years, since she had found in favour of me and felt Carlos was the unfit parent.

The DHHS was meant to be continually monitoring Carlos' behaviour; it was documented by the school that the girls complained their father had been screaming, hitting and throwing things at them but when I asked my lawyer to subpoena the documents between the DHHS and the school they said they wouldn't do it.

The only way I found out what was happening with my girls during this time was when I received the subpoenaed documents released, in August 2015. Carlos' lawyer was ordered to give me all information, including doctor and dentist visits but failed to tell me Loren was admitted into hospital overnight. Even the school principal wrote to me saying I had no parental rights and apparently she had also told that to the children. Carlos didn't have court orders saying he had full custody. The DHHS is a government organisation which has taken my relationship with my daughters away from me, never once interviewing me or investigating the allegations of abuse or Loren and Mandy's relationship with their father.

In August 2015, a Victorian senator came along with me to a DHHS meeting where the representative admitted they had lied in my court

44

reports. The senator was gobsmacked! He said, 'How many other family reports have you done where you have lied?'

I put my trust in professionals who I presumed understood family law and the process but some of them didn't even understand the jurisdiction they were in, because different courts have different jurisdictions, and if you don't have someone representing you who understands 'that court' you're not going to get the right advice or representation.

All up, I spent close to $220,000 in legal fees. That money could've have gone towards Loren and Mandy's future, university, travel, a car for their eighteenth birthdays, anything other than being wasted trying to prove my innocence in a court that took no time or effort to find out the truth. Never in my right mind could I have imagined this would happen me, my friends, and family.

In June 2013, the DHHS made me attend an anger management course. It went for ten weeks and on the third week the coordinator said to me, 'You shouldn't be here, you're not an angry person, if you keep coming though you will turn into one! They signed me out of that class and for the last seven weeks I had one-on-one counselling, but six months later, on Christmas Day 2013, I tried to commit suicide. Glen didn't know that I left early that morning and just lay down on a highway. A lady stopped to help me and she called an ambulance; she too had tried to commit suicide before. It was my first Christmas without my children; it was really hard.

I did try again with the DHHS. I suggested three different clinical psychologists to do the reunification and they said, 'No, we are not going to pay for those, and you aren't either because if you pay they will be biased to your situation.'

When I met with them to do the yearly case plan, they told me they were following the one they already had in place with Carlos, Nerida, and the girls, and I had no say. I asked them about the courtordered therapy and they said, 'No, we are still trying to find the right psychologist to start reunification. Another case plan was created in 2014 and then again in 2015, but I wasn't included because I was painted as a 'trouble-maker'. I'm not a trouble maker; I'm just a mother who misses her kids.

45

I love you girls; I am so sorry you had to go through this pain; I am sorry I married a man like your father; I'm sorry I wasn't five steps ahead so I could see what he was doing to you and to us and I am sorry he took your childhood away.

I hope by telling my story, it will encourage more parents to come forward. I was robbed of a relationship with my daughters. The system failed to see the real person my ex-husband is and ignored the fact that there had never been any history or evidence of violence. I was one of the many real victims of family violence while we were married, but because I didn't report it, apparently that means it never happened. The mental abuse my ex-husband has inflicted on my children to make them not only abandon their best friends, step-brother and sister, but blackmail them into abandoning a relationship with their own mother, will affect them for the rest of their lives. The last time I saw my children they were thirty-plus kilograms overweight, bitter, and still angry. They don't socialise, rarely go out, and still ignore Dee's daughters and their other friends at school. I have fought for as long as I can, I have cried more tears than water in the ocean. No more amount of money or advice will bring them back. It's been six years and a half years now and I have only seen my daughters a total of 37.5 hours. I long for their hugs, laughs, and to be able to be their mum again every day.

LEGAL COMMENTARY

Unfortunately, the existence of family violence, including physical violence, is very clear here. In Sally's description of Carlos, we can also see the potential for mental health concerns, particularly around the instability in his relationship with his family and siblings, which created deep insecurity.

It is common for physical violence to be triggered, or increase, during pregnancy, resulting from jealous or controlling behaviour.

Had Sally reported the violence to the police, then she may have been able to obtain a Safety Notice or intervention order for her personal protection, however, this may also have triggered a separation. It is possible Sally may not have had the emotional support at this time to take such a significant step, had she sought advice from a specialist family lawyer, rather than a 'generalist lawyer' as described by her. Sally should have been advised to consider an intervention order for her personal protection following her separation, noting that she was at substantial risk of further violence during this period, and also of the importance of obtaining parenting orders to confirm the arrangements for the children moving forward. The children may also have been at risk of physical harm, given Carlos' prior conduct.

Whilst parenting orders are not always necessary for all parents who separate, in cases such as this, where there was significant family violence, potential mental health issues for Carlos, and a clearly volatile relationship between Sally and Carlos, they certainly should have been recommended. This may have allowed Sally to establish clear boundaries of behaviour for Carlos, which may have prevented the parental alienation of the children which followed and escalated over time.

Sally's approach to the relationship with Carlos and the children following separation is to be commended in light of the circumstances in her case, and certainly complies with the obligation that exists under the Family Law Act to facilitate and promote a meaningful relationship between them[4]. However, where there is a risk to the physical and psychological welfare of the children, their safety must take priority[5] . If family violence occurs within a child's presence or hearing, or if they witness the aftermath of violence, such as seeing Sally distressed or wounded, then this would have given rise to grounds for an intervention order and would have been a factor to be considered in post-separation parenting arrangements[6].

A significant factor in Sally's story was her decision to increase Carlos' time with the children to equal time, particularly in circumstances where he 'was never really interested in their activities or picked them up on time'. Under the Family Law Act, the court will consider whether equal care should be ordered if both parties are granted parental responsibility for their children[7] . However, contrary to popular belief, shared care is not ordered in most cases; in fact, it is only ordered in a minority of cases. The kind of factors that are typically taken into account in a parenting case, where shared care is sought, include:

- the nature of the relationship between the child and each of the parents.
- the approach to parenting taken by both parents.
- the practicality of the arrangements[8] .

In cases where shared care is ordered, typically children are older in age; the parents reside close to one another and the school; and the parents have an amicable co-parenting relationship. These factors are not apparent in Sally's case, and had she sought legal advice, she may have been advised that Carlos would be entitled to substantial significant time with the children[9] , which includes time during the week and on weekends, of somewhere between three to six nights a fortnight. Further, if it was established that there was a risk for the children in spending time with their father, due to his mental health or family violence, then Carlos may have had his time further reduced, and he may have been required to undertake additional steps such as:

- ongoing therapeutic counselling
- anger management course
- parenting after separation course[10] .

If Sally had commenced parenting proceedings in the context of this case, then a family report[11] would have been ordered as part of those proceedings, with a counsellor/psychologist (either court-appointed or private) to assess the family dynamics, by interviewing both Carlos and

Sally separately, speaking to the children separately, and by observing the children with each parent. As part of the family report process, typically an assessment of risk is undertaken with regard to family violence or mental health issues reported by either party, and then recommendations regarding the time arrangements would be made.

A common trigger in parental alienation cases can be the introduction of a new partner into the family dynamic. In Sally's case, she partnered with Glen approximately four years after separation. Sally suggests that after this time, and after the death of her mother, Carlos' behaviour around the parenting arrangements escalated. Court orders would have prevented this, as it would have set clear boundaries for Carlos' time with the children, which would have been enforceable by Sally. This includes being able to speak to the children by telephone when they were with Carlos, and ensuring the children were returned on time.

Carlos' behaviour the evening before Sally went overseas is significant. It shows a clear escalation of his behaviour, suggesting that court proceedings and parenting orders for Sally were not only warranted, but necessary. It also shows Carlos would take great lengths to assert his control over the children, and the fact that he held the girls to ransom in this way, before a key event in their and Sally's life, indicates that he has little if any insight into the impact of his behaviour on the children. The police clearly gave Sally advice to seek parenting orders to prevent this from happening again. The signs of parental alienation were:

- When Loren asked to spend more time with her father prior to the US holiday
- Loren's comments and attitude the evening before the US holiday
- Loren's comment upon her return to Sally's care: 'I don't know who to believe, YOU or DAD!'
- Glen's suggestion that Sally should check on Mandy: 'She said she's really scared, because in the car, Nerida and Carlos said, 'They know people in high places and as soon as you get home they're going to take us away from you and Mum'.'
- Mandy's comments during the overseas trip that her father was 'really strict and yells at us', and the concern expressed to Aunt Lucy that

49

he might 'break' her American doll, saying, 'That's what he does to anything Mum has bought me, he 'hurts' it'.

• Mandy pleading with her mother, not wanting to return to Carlos following the US trip.

Had Sally sought legal advice from a family lawyer upon her return from the US trip, then she may have been advised to issue parenting proceedings. Had the parental alienation been detected through the family report process, then it is possible that this intervention would have prevented:

• the involvement of the DHHS and the resulting Children's Court proceedings

• the ultimate destruction of the relationship between Sally and her two children.

Even if the DHHS had been involved in the matter, via the notification which had been made by the children's school, in my experience, had family law proceedings been in place at that time, the DHHS may have suspended any action, until the determination of interim applications in the family law system.

It is important to understand that the rules of evidence, and therefore the requirement of proof of allegations of abuse (whether physical, mental, or emotional), in both the Family Law Courts, and the Children's Court are vastly different. The primary source of evidence in parenting disputes in the family law system is via subpoenas, direct evidence from parties, and the family report process, which includes the children being interviewed separately from their parents by an appropriately trained counsellor/psychologist, and then being observed with their parents. Had the children shown genuine affection towards their mother during the family report process, or refused to repeat the allegations of abuse, or indeed explained that their father had influenced them to make the allegations, then this may have exposed and therefore ended Carlos' destructive behaviour. This outcome, though, would have varied depending on when the family report process commenced and the extent of the alienation occurring at that time.

It is clear when reading the description of the court events that transpired for Sally, that when the matter was before the Family Law Courts, the parental alienation was identified, however, when the matter was before the Children's Court, the case was being run on the recommendations of the DHHS workers. It is my experience that many of the DHHS workers are inexperienced, overworked, and under-resourced, which means that there may not have been the time, care, funding, or attention available to investigate beyond what the children had disclosed. This has had an extremely unfortunate outcome for the children, and for Sally.

Sally's decision to sign the twelve-month supervision order, which meant she had to admit to physically abusing her children, was a clear mistake and something she should have been advised against doing. It appears that she felt under duress to sign this document in the hope that she could thereafter unify with Mandy and Loren.

Had this case been conducted in the Family Law Court, then it is my view that the evidence of the allegations would have been rigorously tested, and the parental alienation was more likely to have been identified.

Legal Commentary by Monica Blizzard Accredited Family Law Specialist (LIV)

Kate

Mother of two daughters: Sophie and Louise

Profession: Fitness Professional

Location: Adelaide, South Australia

'We must be willing to let go of the life we've planned,
so as to have the life that is waiting for us.'

- Joseph Campbell

I grew up in the eastern suburbs of Adelaide, in a well-to-do area. Growing up, I felt a strong connection with my father's Barossa German side of the family. They loved playing tennis and while my brother was busy turning pro, I was at home with Mum's Jane Fonda workout video; for the 1980s it was seriously ground-breaking fitness! Mum and Dad always encouraged me to follow my dreams, but when I chose 'working out' as a career path, they were dubious, but I was determined to prove them wrong, and during my final year of high school, I became a certified teacher; even contracting glandular fever didn't stop me! Fitness was in my blood and I loved it.

My parents were married straight out of high school, are still happy, and always active. Dad is an architect who spent his life designing houses and shopping centres, while my mother was a very stylish stay-at-home-mum who was great in the kitchen, two traits I unfortunately didn't inherit. Our family life was fairly stress-free. Dad let me be 'me' and always made time to talk problems through. My younger brother and I were typical squabbling siblings, even though he is one of the funniest and most considerate people I know. Overall, our family bond is strong through thick and thin; we've always been there for each other.

While studying sport science, my boyfriend at the time said he thought I had a good brain for computer programming, so I decided to give it a try. Soon after the course, I found work as a database programmer. I juggled my hours with a part-time job at a gym, which is where I met John. He oozed confidence and charm, was quite cocky at times, but overall he was a good man. His friends say, 'John's great, just ask him, he'll tell you!' After we'd been dating for almost a year, John was transferred to Darwin for a telecommunications project. We decided I would move with him, which was a huge adjustment, but I soon became busy with two jobs; one training people to use computer software and the other as a trainer at a local gym. John's best friend Phil and Phil's wife Jane, came to visit us for a holiday. His wife wanted to treat herself to a ring to celebrate the arrival of their baby, so we went shopping together. While she was looking, I saw one I liked and she immediately said, 'Kate, you HAVE to show John!' Before I knew it, John and I were back in the shop putting the ring on layby. When we walked out, John turned to me and said, 'I guess this means we're engaged?' and I said, 'Yeah, I guess we are.' I was dying to get married and have kids. I was so happy! John was transferred back to Adelaide after a year and within six months of our return we were married, and I was pregnant with our honeymoon baby. I LOVED being pregnant, but the excitement didn't last long because while I was pregnant, John refused to touch me. He said, 'If the situation was reversed, I would have to respect your decision, so when I say 'No' you need to respect that.' Physically and emotionally, my hormones were raging, so him being that way brought me down a lot. His rules, however, didn't seem to apply when we were around his friends; when they hugged or kissed their wives or girlfriends, he would hug and kiss me too.

Our daughter, Sophie, arrived five weeks early, on my last day at work, which was a shock. My parents were living in Perth at the time, but my wonderful mother still managed to catch the first flight to arrive just in time. I was so grateful. Sophie was born healthy but tiny, so after the birth, she was placed in a humidity crib and taken to intensive care. It was hard not having her with me, but we went in every day for cuddles and within weeks she was strong enough to come home. For the first few months, I found myself incapable of thinking of anything other than Sophie. Was she okay? Why is she crying? I struggled to sleep, thinking she might die or be in need of something. When she was awake, I was afraid to put her down. I felt helpless and incapable, yet I didn't trust anyone else to look after her. About three days later, I was on the couch nursing her when a segment on postnatal depression came on the television. A list came up on the screen of the symptoms; I couldn't believe it, that was me! I told John when he came home and all he said was 'Yeah, I already knew that'. His lack of emotional support did make me feel alone, but at least now I knew it was common and I could start working on getting over it. At this time, we were living with John's parents who were lovely and supportive. John and I had sold the flat I owned to secure a down payment for a family home and also to clear a personal loan he had. After six months of house hunting, we found a great place in the Adelaide Hills. Sophie was such a good baby and once I found my feet, I started working as a trainer at the local fitness centre, which allowed me to bring her with me. It also gave me the chance to get to know the local mums and join their playgroup. Our social circle became a fun collection of the mums and dads from the area. Every weekend we would be at someone's house having dinner and drinks while the kids played. It was great. Two years later, our second baby girl, Louise, arrived. She was born with the umbilical cord wrapped around her neck, so when she came out, she was blue and out of breath. John and I watched helplessly as the doctor revived her. Then he placed her in my arms, and, without a sound, she looked up at me and stared.

Louise was a very clingy and cuddly baby. Sophie grew quickly into an imaginative girl who loved princesses and angels, dancing, and styling her outfits. She had the most beautiful, long, blonde, thick hair which she loved putting up in creative ways. Louise constantly had noise coming from her mouth; singing or humming, it only stopped when her mouth was full or if she was asleep. Her favourite game to play was 'Monster'; I'd pretend to be a scary monster, stomping towards her, she'd let out a squeal then run and hide! Even as a crawling baby she loved it, and she and her friends would demand I do it again and again until I was hoarse from doing the 'Monster' voice. At school drop off, Louise's teacher would wait patiently as Louise gave me 'just one more kiss goodbye', some mornings at least a dozen times! Louise was very perceptive and sensitive. I loved her wonderful take on the world. Sophie was more of a daredevil; always performing and trying new things. Together, we would make up routines for her and her friends to perform; build fairy tents; and do treasure hunts in the backyard. She also had real style; mixing and matching her clothes and designing outfits. When Louise was a baby, Sophie would dress her up with clips, ribbons, and scarfs; she'd even style the dogs! I encouraged her independence and unique talents. She was openly emotional, and we would often sit and talk through teary times. She was a brave, sensitive soul who always wanted to please people, especially her father; the girls constantly sought John's approval.

I started exercising every day, as it was great to combat any depressing moments I would have. Little by little I trimmed right down; I have never been given so many compliments in my life and John loved it! When someone would say something, he would affectionately throw his arms around me, like I was his prize, but he was only ever like that in public. Behind closed doors, I could never do anything right. Most nights, he would make his own dinner because he never liked what I cooked, then he'd stomp around the house picking up stuff because tidy was never tidy enough, then he'd sit on the couch drinking beer, or leave to go out to his friend's bar. I'd often have panic attacks that this was how it was going to be for the rest of my life. Over the years, that feeling became too much and I acquired an eating disorder which John later used against me. We did try counselling, but the therapist made me feel like I was the only one with a problem. All I really needed was to be cuddled and loved more.

In 2007, six years after we were married, a new family moved into the neighbourhood, directly across the road from the school. Therese had gorgeous Barbie doll hair, a three-year-old and a baby. Within a week of arriving they threw a lavish party, inviting all of us, and insisting not to bring a thing. It didn't take long for the four of us: Therese, her husband Ben, John, and I to become close. John and Therese were night owls and liked to party, occasionally dabbling in pot, which wasn't Ben's or my thing; we preferred spending our evenings discussing 'life's issues'. Therese's husband, Ben, was a lovely, intelligent, and very successful guy. Therese would often drape herself over John and say, 'You are so lucky, Kate. He's just the best father. We really have won the gold medals with our husbands.' We didn't mind that Therese had to be the centre of attention; she was fullon but fun. I was always the one off to bed first; sometimes the kids would come with me and sometimes they'd fall asleep and stay, and John would stumble home later. One night, after being joined at the hip with our neighbours for eight months, Ben mentioned moving to Dubai. Financially, it would set them up and he could retire at the age of forty. Two months later, in November 2008, Ben did leave, with the thought that Therese and the kids would follow once the house was packed up. As soon as he was gone, it was John's and my job to look after Therese. She would call and say, 'I've got a blue job; I need John to come over now!' At first I thought nothing of it, but the visits became more frequent and he would often stay the night 'on the couch' he said. I trusted him, but I couldn't

57

deny my niggle anymore, so I asked John, 'Do you love me anymore?' and he said, 'No, I was going to tell you next week.' I said, 'So, that's it?' and he said, 'Yeah, I can leave tomorrow if you like?' I said, 'Actually, I'd like you to leave right now.'

I started working on getting over the breakup straight away. I bought self-help tapes and listened to them constantly. I was scared and hurt but not being under his control suddenly lifted a burden I had no idea I was carrying. A week after he left, we told the girls. I will never forget the look on Sophie's face; she understood it so much more than Louise.

John told our friends and family he was staying at his parents' house, but when I called, they said they didn't know where he was. The kids told me John was parking his car around the back of Therese's house because it was safer there than on the street. Therese went around telling everyone she had to leave Ben because he had been emotionally and physically abusive; Ben was still in Dubai and had no idea what was happening. At first, our friends said they didn't want to take sides, but they all eventually took hers after knowing me for seven years and her for not even one. One mum said, 'When a couple separates, married women normally turn on the single woman to protect their husbands.' I couldn't believe what I was hearing. I was gutted. I ended up (out of pure frustration) telling off some of the mums at school, which didn't go well. No one wanted to hear the truth. One mum even said, 'It's not Therese's fault.' I pointed across the road to John's car and said, 'But that's his car right there, can't you see it?' The proof was right there and she still said, 'I'm sure they are just good friends.' A few months later, I wrote an email to Ben because I had a feeling he didn't know what was going on. He wrote in his reply: On my last visit home, I found men's underwear that wasn't mine, but Therese denied being with anyone else. Even though John had been living with her for months, she continued to assure Ben she loved him and was still moving to Dubai.

For the first few years, the girls and I maintained our beautiful close relationships. John and I had made a verbal agreement; he had the girls two nights a week and for half the school holidays, but over time it slowly became all about what he wanted; changes to nights at the last minute, but if I asked for an extra hour or a different night, he would send me abusive

58

emails putting my mothering skills down and insisting he have extra time. The girls told me, 'Therese calls you 'dumb dumb' and she says we have a second mummy now, and when we leave, Daddy cries.' The girls never saw these supposed tears John had. One Mother's Day, I received two emails, minutes apart; the subject said: 'Happy Mother's Day, read your email.' The other was over thirty paragraphs of abuse including quotes from the Bible and likening me to a mother who was happy to murder her baby.

For years, I received countless text messages, emails, even tips on what to feed my own children! I also found out that John had maxed out our mortgage before he left. I was paying for everything, while he was still earning a six-figure wage and Therese was a self-declared multi-millionaire. They would deposit a small amount of money into my bank account for the 'Angels' then a separate amount for 'Lucifer' (my code name) then the following month not pay at all. It became so stressful; I had to get the Child Support Agency involved. After an investigation, they found he had been misleading them and demanded he back-pay me. I was so relieved, but in doing this, I woke the sleeping giant.

The week before the 2013 Easter long weekend, (a few weeks after the child support drama) the girls arrived home, saying, 'Dad told us we have to choose between you and him for Easter and we choose you! We want to spend Easter with you, Mum!' I was so relieved and excited and after a great weekend together, I felt reassured our bonds were stronger than ever. Then when we arrived at the handover to meet John, Therese was there instead. We saw her walking along with her two children, so I pulled up beside her and all of a sudden she shouted, 'effing psycho!' I stopped the car and said, 'What did you say?' and she said, 'You heard me. You're an effing psycho!' As I parked the car, she continued to swear at me as she pushed her kids on the swings. I waited till she took a breath then foolishly asked, 'Why do you think I'm a psycho?'. Of course, she had no reason; anytime you'd ask for details or proof of something she'd just jump to another accusation—I'm a slut and sleep around, which is rich when she was the one who stole my husband! Then she grabbed her boobs and jumped up and down saying, 'I don't call doing this for fifteen dollars an hour a job! Why don't you get a real job and stop taking all John's money?'

I said, 'You've never worked a day in your life' and she said 'I don't need to, I'm a multi-millionaire. You need to get yourself a real job.' Then she said my kids hated me, that was the worst thing she said. I remember them just standing there, staring into space. I said, 'That's enough! I will personally take the girls to your place when John gets home' and ushered them away from her. Therese screamed, 'If you take those kids, I will kill you!' launching herself at me and throwing her hands around my throat. I'll never forget looking back at Sophie's little face, frozen, in shock; they were both terrified. We pulled and pushed each other until I managed to pin her down so she would stop. A man came over to break it up, telling us to go back to our children but Therese refused. Sophie was crying, saying, 'I don't know what to do, I want to see Dad.' I said, 'Everything's fine, of course you can see your dad, don't worry,' Therese insisted the girls leave with her and in the end they did want to which totally broke my heart. I pleaded with her to let me speak to them for a few minutes before they left and she said, 'No, get away from them, you're evil.' I had nothing left. I stood there and watched them walk away with her. I don't know how long I stayed in the park, sobbing. I was so humiliated. I had never been in that sort of situation before, so I didn't know what to do. I called the police, but they said they were too busy to come out. My parents lived around the corner, so after a while, I picked myself up and drove there. When they opened the door, I collapsed. Dad calmed me down then advised me to write a short and long statement to take to the police, but when we arrived, the officer refused to take my statement saying we had to wait for the officers who had already been assigned to the case to come back. An hour later, two female police officers took us into an interview room. I sat there, like a victim from a cop show, chunks of my hair missing, cuts on my face, and my top torn and dirty. They allowed me to tell my side of the story then when I finished they said, 'We are arresting you for assault.' My jaw hit the floor. Dad said, 'How is that possible?' They said they had already interviewed Therese and the girls and when they arrived; she was hysterical and had to call an ambulance. I said, 'But I was the one who called you to report it and I gave you her name.' Then I pointed to my top and they said, 'How do we know you didn't do that yourself?' Apparently, my girls were worried about Therese and that's why they initially thought I was to blame, but once I had a chance to explain it properly, they soon realised it was a domestic incident and that Therese was, in fact, the crazy one. They let me go, strongly advising me to find a good lawyer.

The police didn't hand their report in until the day of our court hearing. The psychologist said the girls were too traumatised to talk about it and no one in the park came forward to be a witness. I also heard that Therese pretended to faint in front of the police and when the ambulance arrived there was nothing for them to do, so they left. Two days later, I went to school to pick up the girls, and a work colleague offered to come with me because I was worried there might be another confrontation. When we arrived, they weren't there. John sent me a text saying: The children will not be attending school, we are keeping them here until we take you to court. I totally lost it. My friend and I went to the police station, but there was nothing they could do. Therese had put a restraining order on me and had charged me with assault. I was recommended a lawyer, but he really stuffed me around. I paid $5,000 upfront then he organised a psychologist who was truly awful. She decided after a month the girls were still too traumatised to see me. I asked if I could have more information on how they were going and she firmly said, 'No, you can't ask!' I was so shocked. I started sobbing, then when I stood up, my legs came out from under me. I tried to move them, but they were like jelly. Dad had to throw his arms under me to help me up. My lawyer's office was on the floor above, so we called him straight away. When we arrived the receptionist said, 'We can't continue to legally advise you until you pay another $5,000.' Dad and I stood there not sure what to say. We weren't even allowed to ask him why the psychologist had acted the way she had. All he had done was prepare a document so I could sue for custody (which was so poorly done it had to be rewritten) and set up a meeting with the awful psychologist from upstairs, all for five grand! I was in trouble financially, so my dad lent me some of my inheritance to pay for the next lawyer. This one was also a barrister and seemed lovely but soon went cold after I paid her, bluntly telling me it could take at least eighteen months to go to trial and even then I probably wouldn't get custody of the children. I knew she didn't believe me, so I gave her a booklet my youngest made for me just before I stopped seeing them. On the cover it said, 'Why I love my mum'. It was the most beautiful thing.

At the first hearing, my barrister made me sit outside, then appeared with papers for me to sign, saying that because I still had the assault charge on me, I had to sign the documents to proceed. My partner, brother, and I divided it up quickly to try and read it properly, but she kept hurrying me up so the court could go to lunch. In the end, she convinced me I had no other choice, so I signed it. Soon after, I decided to close my account with her and contact the lawyer who had done our separation. When I received all my paperwork, my daughters' booklet was missing, and I never got it back.

When my new lawyer read the documents I was made to sign, she was dumbfounded. 'Why did you sign this? You've signed all your rights away!' I had no idea. Apparently, I had signed all my parental rights over to John and was happy to not see or speak to my kids, even if I saw them in public. It had also pushed my case back further; she immediately went to work to get me back on track. I explained I only had $50,000 in total to spend; that was all my father could afford to lose. I took a little comfort in knowing it was my inheritance, and unfortunately that amount only lasted three months. When it ran out, they said, 'It's a shame we have to leave you now.' All they wanted was money. The barrister I had was wonderful, though, and helped me get legal aid. At the Magistrates Court, she recommended we go to the Family Court because it would be much quicker, and it was. During this time, they also conducted two family psychology assessments which in summary claimed: 'It wasn't alienation, the kids were clearly traumatised and their mother must have done something to make them act this way.' Both reports recommended I don't see my kids. I was breaking down often at work and had to take a lot of time off to go to appointments and attend court. I was only seeing the girls once a fortnight, supervised and only if they wanted to see me. At first they did, but only for ten minutes; other times, Sophie would come but Louise refused to, then eventually both of them refused. The 'experts' told me, 'this is how the process works' but as soon as they knew they didn't have to see me, they were gone. The whole court process took over two years and in the end, the legal aid lawyer said they would no longer fund me if I didn't agree to their mediation custody proposal. I walked away with access of one night a fortnight.

During the visits, the girls became more and more distant; they wouldn't hug me, smile, or communicate. Sometimes, they would forget, and I would see glimpses of their old selves. They also behaved this way to my family; their beloved Nanny, Poppa, and their Uncle Pete. They were also distant to our dogs, who were confused and gave up going to them for affection. It had been two years since they had seen them and for them to behave like aliens was heartbreaking. We did everything we could to keep it light and non-confrontational, but each visit became harder and harder. I did try to apologise for what happened at the park, tell them how sorry I was, and remind them that 'Therese ran to me, remember? I was standing there with you' but they both sat there silent and uncomfortable, so I haven't bought it up since.

Christmas 2015, I was due to have the girls for three nights, but when I arrived at the pick-up point, the police were there instead to arrest me. Therese and John had claimed they had video footage of me driving past their house making rude gestures. Their house is on a main road and on my way to work. There is a back way, along a windy road which I often take but in bad weather it's dangerous. I sent a text to John asking where the girls were and he replied, 'You don't get to see them because you've been arrested.' It was the day before Christmas. I had to go to court for that. The judge said, 'She can drive on the road, it's a main road, it's fine, it makes sense.' Even after the court ruling, Therese tried again to have me arrested for driving by. It is now officially on police records recorded that Therese is 'mischievous, inconveniences police officers, and anything she reports in the future is to be treated sceptically'. Hearing that was a big win.

From July 2016, I saw the girls two nights a fortnight. I would pick them up Friday and we would spend the weekend together, but they never wanted to be there. My youngest just sat in silence, staring off into the distance. There is no more 'scary monster' playing, singing, or funny noises coming from my little Louise, and Sophie doesn't dance anymore or play dress-ups. Therese doesn't allow Sophie to dress herself and hates it if her outfits don't match. Louise once told me that Sophie had a meltdown because Therese said, 'If you don't put this outfit on, I'll cut your hair off, like a boy!'

New Year's Day 2017, I had a night allocated to me, but when I arrived, they refused to leave with me. John just stood there as they told me that I scare them, and that Louise was so afraid she'd been throwing up all morning. Then they both said, 'We don't want to see you.' I asked John, 'Why?' and he said, 'What can I do, if that's how they feel? Perhaps you need to take a good hard look at yourself.' Four weeks later, I picked them up for a fournight stay, but they said they would only stay for a few hours. I bought them a book each, and lunch, and sat them down to tell them I loved them with all my heart and would be there in a heartbeat if they ever needed me, but they can't treat me and their grandparents like this anymore. We all love them, but until they actually want a relationship with us, it will never work. I told them I could see the stress they were under and that I didn't want them to feel like that anymore. They listened and nodded then I reiterated that I loved them and would always be there for them if they want to reconnect.

My decision may sound strange but being constantly rejected by them was so hurtful and immensely stressful. They had been taught how to disrespect me and my family and I could see how much stress they were under to constantly play that role. I miss them shockingly and frequently get hit with waves of sadness, especially on school holidays.

I have learnt that nothing hurts quite like being a mother who isn't allowed to be a mother and the awful public stigma of being a woman who has lost her children. I have true friends, but I see many others who don't know me thinking I must have done something to deserve this. The legal system let me down. No one cared that I was an innocent mother desperately wanting her children back. Especially repellent, were the psychological professionals chosen to judge whether I was worthy of having time with my own flesh and blood. They had little empathy and made uneducated judgements which changed the course of my life, and my children's lives, forever. It was truly horrific.

Nowadays, I try to be a little more selfish every day. It feels wrong, but I have to in order to survive. The more I do for myself, the better I feel. I hope when my girls are older and leave home they will have a clearer perspective on life. I really hope they are able to follow what they want in life, allow themselves to play again, and let their gorgeous personalities shine through. I really hope they do that. My parents have struggled a lot since I lost the girls, but we are closer than ever, which I am grateful for. I hope one day I will share that same bond with my girls.

WORDS FROM NANNY

(MY MUM)

It has been six long, torturous years, watching my two granddaughters go from happy, carefree, loving children to cold, unsmiling, and robotic in my company and that of any of our relatives. Earlier on, there were glimpses of the children I once knew, but over time they became less and less. To me, it's like they've died, but my grieving has never stopped. I think of them every day, wondering how they are and what they are doing. On top of that, I have had to watch my daughter go through this nightmare where her ex and his partner waged a never-ending war of slander and defamation, which has created another layer of grief and anxiety, resulting in sleepless nights, fatigue, and depression, I find it difficult to explain. I don't think enough consideration is given to the alienated parent; they are the ones who are the real victims, and the children are the pawns.

WORDS FROM POPPA

(MY DAD)

The other day, my local GP asked me if I had any grandchildren. Without thinking, I immediately responded, 'No, I don't!' My wife quickly nudged me and said, 'You do so! Do you realise what you said?' That was six years after the whole insidious process started. Gone. Shadows of the loving grandchildren we had shared our lives with. As a man, I rationalise the futility of our endeavour to save the girls. Mediators, lawyers, and psychologists. The people who should know better, or at least act with a depth of understanding, don't. They stand in attendance like traffic police and watch to make sure due process is followed without a thought that the children, through no fault of their own, are mentally damaged for life. There is no comfort for us. Our hopes and dreams of watching and sharing in the lives of our grandchildren have been ripped out of our hearts. It is that dramatic and devastating. Nobody, other than those who have gone through this before, have any comprehension. Society only seems capable of a genuine look of dismay or a sympathetic, 'How terrible!'. When we think how devastating the loss of the children is for our daughter, we know our pain could be so much more.

Thank you for reading my story.

Happiness and love to you and your family - Kate

LEGAL COMMENTARY

Although there was no obvious family violence occurring in Kate's marriage, there were red flags in John's behaviour, including his refusing to touch her whilst she was pregnant and being overly critical of her, resulting in her developing an eating disorder.

Kate doesn't mention seeking legal advice immediately after their separation, and confirms that their parenting arrangements were only agreed verbally. This meant that when John started to control them—changing arrangements at the last minute or seeking additional time—there was no accountability or enforceability for him. In doing so, and by sending abusive emails, he was able to pressure her to into agreeing to the changes.

His abusive emails and text messages could have formed the basis for Kate to have sought an intervention order against John, to prevent this behaviour. At this time, if Kate had sought legal advice from a family lawyer, she may also have been advised to obtain parenting orders to ensure stability for the children.

The commencement of parental alienation of the children by John against Kate, can be seen in their comments 'Therese calls you dumb dumb' and to having 'a second mummy now'. It can also be seen to the reference of 'when we leave, Daddy cries', and the reference to naming Kate 'Lucifer' in bank transactions. This is evidence of manipulation of the children against their mother. Kate's comments about their financial arrangements are also cause for concern. It seems, from her description of the mortgage being 'maxed out', that she may not have sought legal advice concerning her property settlement entitlements, and that John was not paying child support. This could have been identified as financial abuse, which also comes within the definition of family violence, and could also form the basis of an application for an intervention order, or a breach of any existing order.

A breach of an intervention order can result in the perpetrator being jailed. This threat can be a powerful influence in curbing behaviour of this kind for separated parties.

Kate's description of her interaction with Therese, which included verbal abuse and physical violence (and potentially attempted strangulation), and which took place in front of the children, has exposed the children to violence, and under the law, this could have had significant consequences on their wellbeing, and the future parenting arrangements for the children, in being exposed to such behaviour. Arguably, had Kate reported the incident to the police first, sought family law legal advice, and obtained an intervention order, then Therese may have been prevented from coming into contact with the children and Kate. Kate's decision not to remove the children from the situation and from Therese had a significant consequence. Once the children were in Therese's control, she and John were able to use this to their advantage and withhold the children from Kate.

In this day and age, and with the technology we have available via our smartphones, I will often advise a client to record or video an incident, or the aftermath of an incident, in full view of the other party, as proof of what has transpired. This can often be a key part of the case, or act as a deterrent to a party taking legal action or reporting the matter to the police[12] .There may otherwise be CCTV available in public areas, and if there are concerns about the potential behaviours of the other party, it is important that the location of changeover is secure. Had there been any recorded evidence of what transpired, then this could have been produced under court subpoena and may have prevented the outcome in Kate's case, and the alienation of her children. Kate should have sought specialist family law advice immediately after the incident with Therese, as part of such an application she could have:

- sought the immediate return of the children to her care via a recovery order[13] .
- sought an intervention order against both John and Therese, based on their behaviour[14] .

- obtained a family report to assess the trauma to the children and expose any parental alienation that may have been occurring.

The delay in taking action meant the children were exposed for an extended period to the influence of John and Therese, thereby creating a 'status quo' in parenting arrangements which can be difficult to shift.

There did not appear to be any basis for Kate to have supervised time with the children, and it is unclear what documents she signed which effectively 'signed her rights away'. Unfortunately, it seems that Kate did not receive adequate legal representation during this time.

Kate mentions that the eventual court hearing took two years to be finalised, and during that time she had minimal contact with her children. Two years for John and Therese to alienate the children from her. Kate's description of the children being distant and uncommunicative is evidence of the impact the influence had on them.

Legal Commentary by Monica Blizzard Accredited Family Law Specialist (LIV)

POETRY AND LYRICS

Mum's the Word

In normal circumstances
Mums the word
But in our case
We're neither seen, nor heard.

Still, we keep trying
Longing keeps us spurred
The thought of our children
Means we are undeterred.

Always hopeful
The tide will turn
And that light bulb moment
Will lead to our children returned.

Our children think
They have been spurned
That we no longer care
Whilst our hearts are churned.

This life we live
The lies that are transferred
From the guilty parent
Our protestations deferred.

Compliance is demanded
Secrets are conferred
Don't give anything away kid
Mums the word!

By Andrea Walker (UK)

THE GATE-KEEPER'S TRAP

A child so green, manipulation not seen
To him they act sweet, to you, cold and mean.
Kid just sees the surface, the gifts, the fun
If they buy him enough, he won't miss his mum.
Well, that's what they think as they parade him with pride
Like champion horse trainers, but he's broken inside.
But he'll bury it deep, and keep it within
After all, they will brag of what they've done for him.
Like giving him all he could ever need
But it comes with big pressure, obligation, and greed.

No such thing as free lunch, some people do say
When not paid all they want, they will take it away.
And what is the cost to the innocent and young?
A life with scheming puppeteers, and not with their mum.
'Look at all we've given' they're likely to say
When far greater is all that they've taken away.
Years of love and lost time from she who truly cares
Love's not possessive. Love should be shared.
He knows that deep down but there just was no choice
As they covered his mouth and stifled his voice.
To stay in their church, he must sing with their choir
To think of mum was a sin, a blasphemous desire.

Don't rock the boat, dear son or daughter
Unless you are sure you can walk on water.
For now, best remain where you feel you are safe
For to risk all you know takes an eternity of faith.
But the miracle of love for a son or daughter
Is that mums will walk on hot coals,
and on glass, not just water.
They will do all this and let you love who you choose
She would rather win-win, they would rather lose-lose.

by Annie Stanford (Aus)

Darling I miss you

Darling, miss you,
Those words aren't true.
Careful what they tell you,
Seems nothing I can do.
And the lies go around and around,
And my heart's on the ground, it's true.
And I'm missing you so and you don't even know how,
I ache and I cry for you.
And I'm boxed in a cage inside feeling rage that
my child can be kept from me.
But I must keep that feeling down, wear a smile not a frown,
act different to what I feel.
For any mistake, they will surely celebrate and convince you
I'm crazy for real.
Their aim is clear. They're keeping you so near,
filling you with hate and fear.
Vindictive eyes, they can't see compromise or damage
to a child so dear.
They act so unkind but cannot break the bind,
or the link that lies deep within our souls.
He must win the game so I take all the
blame for the false story that he controls.
They've surrounded you and I just can't get through,
for the gate's nearly closed in your mind.

But one day you will see when you turn the right key,
my love was waiting here for you to find.
Darling miss you,
I'm hoping one day soon, you'll find another point of view.
Pushed out! Broken! Squeezed out of my own life.
Insults spoken to a mother and a wife.
Crying, shaking, as he screams all that I lack.
Child's mind is taken, right behind my back.

Gas-lighting then fighting. Not long'til that black dog's biting!
You belittle me, my esteem is zero,
So why are you seen as a hero?

Seems compassion's out of fashion,
Kindness given like a ration.
Go ballistic with narcissistic tendencies,
(you're such a critic!)
Silly me, empathy is now seen as.......em?........pathetic!
(What goes on behind closed doors,
stays behind closed doors)...
No more!

Lyrics by Annie Stanford

Fiona

Mother of two daughters, Pip and Millie

Profession: Product designer

Location: Melbourne, Victoria

'I wish them love,

I wish them happiness,

I wish them health,

I wish their dreams come true.'

- Fiona.

I never dreamed of having a house with a white picket fence, three kids, and a golden retriever, but I did always assume I'd get married and have kids. All I ever aspired for was to have a husband who loved me and children I adored. When I was younger, I studied early childhood development and spent time working with kids, both disabled and in the kindergarten system, so I was never under any delusion that it was going to be easy. I just never realised that putting a father's psyche into the equation would make things so hard.

During my final year at school, my parents' marriage broke down. I can only remember a few altercations between Mum and Dad during my high school years. Looking back, I think I was too busy with my social life to notice what was going on. I was surprised by how much it devastated me. They had been together since they were very young, so I think I just presumed they would stay together. I remember sobbing and asking my boyfriend at the time, 'What happened to happily ever after?' It was then I realised that fairy tales don't always come true.

I did marry in my twenties to a lovely man. We dated for ten years but were only married for eighteen months. He was a great guy who worked long hours then spent most weekends at the football or playing golf. I was lonely and frustrated waiting for him to notice me. Then I met Mal. He made me feel alive again. We would stay up all night talking about life, the world. He valued spending time with me and was interested in hearing my opinions. We both dreamed of travel and adventures, exploring the world and all its diversities. I felt like I was blossoming again and had met someone who was like-minded and believed in the same things.

The first couple of years, we were extremely happy. We both loved our jobs and would look forward to coming home at night to each other. We planned a trip to Morocco, France, Spain, and the United Kingdom; our first adventure together! It was a fantastic trip. Just before we were due to come home, I found out I was pregnant. We had talked about having kids, but it still came as a surprise. We were both thrilled.

Nine months later, Pip was born. She was this amazing little being. We couldn't believe we had made her! She was a very content baby, and as happy as she made me, I struggled being home all the time. I had always worked—I was even working the day I went into labour—so after five weeks, I decided to start a new business selling natural body products. I could work from home and manage it while Pip slept. Mal was also self-employed at the time, selling homewares, so he could be flexible if I needed help. Mal always made an effort to be around as much as possible, but the more involved he became, the more I felt like I was being pushed aside. He began to criticise how I looked after Pip, complaining if I wasn't doing things how he wanted them to be done and saying I was working too much and neglecting her. In fact, it was quite the opposite. Pip and I would have a lovely time together during the day, we would go walking and to the park, visit grandma, read, and sing together.

For the next few years, we both did our best to juggle work and Pip. Mal had made it clear he didn't like that I had the distraction of my business, but it was building momentum and making money. He clearly only wanted me to stay home to tend to the house, cook meals, and look after Pip. When Pip was around two-and-a-half, we discussed having another baby. We thought it would be nice for her to have a sibling and she was becoming quite independent, could dress herself, and clearly vocalise her needs. During my second pregnancy, Mal decided he would take over the family finances. I was experiencing small bouts of forgetfulness, so I was happy for Mal to take over paying the bills. All our money went into a joint account which he managed. I never saw any bank statements nor had access to the account. He would just give me money for housekeeping every Friday.

About a year later, when our second daughter Millie was born, I began to feel overwhelmed. Sometimes, I struggled to get out of bed, was always tired, but having trouble sleeping. I also cried a lot. Later, my doctor suggested to me that I most likely had been struggling with postnatal depression. I thought at the time that I was just having trouble adjusting to the change and more responsibilities and was just extremely tired, like all mothers of young children. I believed we were so lucky. We had each other and two perfect, happy, and healthy girls. I had so much to be grateful for. Mal was a great help with the girls and both grandmothers were always wanting to help out. It was about this time that Mal always seemed to be saying we had no money. I was confused by this because I knew we had money coming in from both our businesses and we were not spending extravagantly. I remember saying to a girlfriend, 'I just don't know where the money is going?'

Then our front gate went missing just before Mal was due to go overseas. It was really strange. The police suggested that someone had stolen it for their own house, so I just thought, Okay. While Mal was away, he insisted that the girls and I stay in Mt Martha (about an hour and a half out of Melbourne) with his mum and dad until he came home. That was really inconvenient for me because I had to drive up to Melbourne every day for daycare so I could keep working. A few days after Mal came home, the gate was hanging back in its place but the word 'cunt' had been laser-cut into it. Mal's homeware business included laser-cut mirrors and he said that his current laser-cutter guy had gone psycho. I was a little frightened. I later found out it was because Mal hadn't been paying his bills. He never admitted to it.

Another strange incident occurred when Mal organised for a female celebrity friend of his to endorse my business of bath and body products. She loaned us $27,000 to exhibit at the Hong Kong trade show so we could grow the customer base for the business. I felt really honoured to be offered the opportunity and made sure I gave Mal the money to repay her as soon as I could, but a few months later, they were waiting for us when we arrived home. She demanded her money back. The boyfriend started screaming at Mal and told me and Millie to get back inside. After they left, Mal told me the boyfriend had an issue with something else and that it had nothing to do with money.

In 2004, when picking Millie up from daycare, one of the assistants commented that she had run into Mal having coffee at our local café with one of the other mothers. I didn't think anything of it. Then, at the daycare centre end of year party at the local park, I mistakenly got confused and we went to the wrong one. Mal went ballistic at me, screaming that I was hopeless and never could get anything right. I had no idea what his problem was. There were not many parks in the area, so we found the correct one not too long after. We all had a fun afternoon and we ended up being the last to leave, chatting with another couple, while our kids played.

In March 2005, I headed off overseas for a business trip. Mal was looking after the girls with the help of both grandmothers. When I returned home, Mal insisted on taking me out for dinner. At dinner, he told me he was leaving me. Ironically, we ended up having a nice night and when we got home, I presumed he'd changed his mind. At that time, we were all living in an inner city two-bedroom house and really needed more space. Friends of ours had a beautiful house nearby on a large block of land. They had built a second house out the back and were planning to sell the front house. I realised Mal hadn't changed his mind and still wanted to separate, when he arranged for the girls and me to move into their front house for six months while they waited for the right time to sell. The strange thing was when we moved in, he moved in too! It was awful; he would disappear for hours, be out all night, or completely ignore me.

We had a holiday to Bali booked months before we moved, but it was pretty clear we weren't going. Mal ended up going on his own and while he was away, I found out about Ally. She was the mother from the café and daycare Christmas party. It now made sense why Mal was so angry at me in the car.

While Mal was in Bali, I packed his things into his car and when he came home, he finally moved out. He told me he had no choice but to leave and it was all my fault. He accused me of not being a good mother and told me I was a horrible and selfish person who he couldn't see a single redeeming quality in. He repeatedly told me he was going to take the girls off me. I remember asking him if I had ever done anything right. He replied by saying the only thing he could think of was that I was really good at celebrating birthdays! I guess when you keep getting told you're a waste of a person you eventually start believing it. I was a total mess. My doctor pointed out that I had the demeanour of someone in an abusive relationship and gave me antidepressants. I closed down both my businesses and just tried to keep it together day-to-day. I was so angry at myself for being stupid enough to believe everything Mal had said to me.

Over the next few months, Mal did make an effort to make sure I was okay, maybe out of guilt or he wanted to look like he was supportive of me to the outside world. He proposed to look after me financially until I got back on my feet, and also pay for all the girls' health, education, and related expenses; he even offered to still pay me half the royalties from two products he had created when we were still together, and half of the proceeds—should he choose to sell them. We also put a parenting agreement in place: three days, two days, two days, because neither of us wanted to spend a whole week away from the girls. All of this was organised via email between us. We never married, so as a de facto couple, we didn't have to go to court.

In 2006, I moved into a rental house in St Kilda. Mal had promised to pay the rent for the first year, but by July 2007 he was $11,500 overdue. He consistently told me he'd paid the rent. The landlord lived overseas, so I had little contact with him. Finally, the landlord told me I had to pay the full amount, or he would have to ask the girls and I to leave. I was crushed, I didn't have that sort of money: I was living week to week. When I asked Mal to pay, he basically told me to shove it. He wasn't interested in keeping his promise to pay the rent for the first year, nor did he care about us being kicked out. I was beside myself, I called Mal's mother to ask her if she would speak to Mal and she told me to sort it out myself, saying that it was my problem, not hers. Then I found out my grandmother had left me $10,000 in her will. It was such a relief. I paid the landlord with the whole amount and negotiated to pay the remainder in instalments. I realised that I had to speak to a lawyer to have our agreements legally binding.

The lawyers' recommendation was to stop trusting Mal immediately and to make sure I had the girls in my care when Mal was served the documents, just to be safe. Directly after my meeting with the lawyer, I didn't wait for school to finish, I went straight to Pip's school to pick her up, but when I arrived, Mal was there. Pip's teacher intervened and calmed both of us down, saying it would be too distressing for Pip if we caused a scene, so we both left without her. How did Mal know I was going to the school? He always seemed to know exactly where I was and what I did. My suspicion was confirmed after speaking with a mutual friend Mal had had my phone tapped after we separated.

Over the next few years, Mal was sent letters from my lawyers regarding finalising custody and financial matters, but he ignored every one, leaving me no further advanced and stuck with legal fees.

One day, I got a call from my old contract manufacturer's daughter. I had helped her start her own business, and she wanted to offer me a job helping her and her partner with their private label and brand business. This was perfect because the hours were flexible and I could work from home, which meant I was still there for the girls.

Mal's payments of the school fees were long overdue. The school regularly followed it up, copying me in on emails with threats the girls would be withheld from attending until the fees were paid. He would often try to bully and guilt me into paying half the school fees, and I started to wonder if there had been money when Mal said there wasn't. I had access to my earnings from my businesses through my contract manufacturer. I was obtaining the orders for bath and body products that were exported to America, and he was producing and sending. When he received payment for the orders, he paid me my fee. As such, I had commission statements from him. I had been making great money. I soon discovered Mal had been ringing him claiming we were short and organising advances. As he was my partner, my contract manufacturer never questioned his request. I kept this information to myself until I saw Mal and the topic of the school fees came up again, then I took the opportunity to ask, 'Remember all that money you stole from me? Wouldn't that cover my share of the school fees?' He was shocked, speechless. I knew by the look on his face, he was guilty.

A few years later, when Pip was ten and Millie was six, I met my now-partner, Cam, who I didn't officially introduce to the girls for six months. Cam and I waited until we had been together for almost a year before he moved in. The girls absolutely loved him. Most mornings, Millie would climb into our bed for a cuddle, even when Cam would say, 'This bed isn't big enough for three!' Millie would say, 'Okay, you can sleep in my bed then!' The same day I told Mal that Cam was moving in, he proposed to his girlfriend of six weeks, Kim. He always tried to outdo me! We then met for coffee and Mal agreed to have the settlement and custody terms written up, but once I got the plan drawn up, he refused to sign them, saying he didn't feel the need to formalise our agreement. Again, I was left with the lawyers' fees and no papers signed. Years went by with the animosity between us unchanging.

In 2010, Mal moved the girls to another school without my consent. Pip had finished Grade 6 and was looking forward to going to high school, adjacent to the primary school she was already attending. She had even done the orientation day for Grade Seven already. Millie was still in primary school. Mal seemed to think he could make a huge decision, like deciding the girls' education, unilaterally, without consulting my thoughts. He also knew very clearly that my preference was for the girls to go to an all-girl school.

Mal and I chose to communicate by email when it came to the girls, and I could always tell when he was having a hard time, because I would get abusive texts and a barrage of tirades. I knew something was up when they all moved to Mount Martha into Mal's mother's house, an hour out of town on the coast. This was taxing on the girls because it meant their day was so much longer, getting up early and not getting back to their grandmother's until late, and some afternoons they would have sporting commitments, so by the time they'd get home they were exhausted. Cam and I lived around the corner from the school, so I suggested to Mal the girls stay with us until he was settled. I even suggested he have weekends instead. He told me the girls were coping fine and the travelling didn't bother them at all, but I could tell the girls were being compromised and worn down by it all.

Slowly, over time, the girls started to shut down. They became uncooperative. They stopped doing little things like making their beds, carrying their dishes to the sink, and hanging their towels up in the bathroom. Their manners were slowly vanishing, and we were fighting a lot. They were coming back from the week at Mal's unsettled and with attitude. It would then take them a few days to begin behaving like the happy girls we knew, then the cycle would happen again. It was challenging trying to juggle their moods because they seemed to disregard everything I'd say, but they were teenagers, after all. Then one day before I was to pick the girls up for our week together, I got an email from Mal saying the kids didn't want to come home with me because they didn't feel comfortable. I was astounded; I could not believe what he was doing. Our custody arrangements had been in place for many years now, and Cam and I had agreed the girls could spend a little more time with Mal if that's what they wanted, but only if we saw them over the weekend to talk to them about what was going on. Mal declined this. I also suggested that if he was unhappy with the current week-on-week-off arrangement, then we could all sit down with a court-appointed mediator and formalise a new custody arrangement, but he was still uncooperative.

I contacted a family lawyer again, and nine years after we separated, we finally ended up in court. It was a truly traumatic and very sad time, and we only had limited access with the girls leading up to the hearing. When we did see them, they were very happy to be home, chatty, engaging, and affectionate. On advice from my lawyer, I broached the subject of going back to our week-on-week-off arrangement. The response I got was extraordinary. They both froze up, wouldn't make eye contact, and completely shut down. Pip just keep mentioning 'the lawyer'. Cam and I got the feeling they had been instructed not to speak to us, and Mal had used the lawyer as a reason why.

As part of the legal negotiations, we all attended a session with a clinical psychologist whose specialty was in the fields of conflict resolution and family therapy. She saw each of the children, then Mal and myself separately, and observed how each household interacted as a family; Cam and I, then Mal and Kim, Mal's new wife, participating. The results of the report were stunning. It took a little time to get the report released, as Mal would not pay his portion of the fee, then he dismissed his lawyer. Finally, the results were published, and they took me by total surprise. The doctor certainly pointed out that I was not perfect and possibly on occasion my actions—although normal—were reactive and unsuitable, and I need to develop strategies for better communication with the girls.

But it was her evaluation of Mal that floored me:

There is no doubt in the writer's mind that the father's hatred of the mother is deep, intense, and fixed, and that he thinks she a bad mother to the point where he had nothing positive to say about her at all; and he made this profoundly obvious to the children, to the school, and I suspect anyone who meets him. It seems to permeate everything he says and does.

It is also clear to the writer that the father is sharing a great deal of inappropriate information and stories about the mother with the children, and that he has done, and still continues to denigrate and undermine the mother.

The father is clearly entrenched in and motivated to demonise and vilify the mother, and to undermine her, to denigrate her and to paint her as the villain and himself and the children as the victims, and to encourage the children to have similar views and to, in fact, reject and/or alienate the mother for his own purposes, reasons and needs.

It appears to have resulted in the children's beliefs and thoughts almost becoming contaminated by the father's prevailing negative opinion of the mother, and there is a heavy reliance upon borrowed scenarios that have been told to them that they present as face, but they seem unable to provide any realistic or consistent basis for how they feel or how they came to these beliefs.

The psychologist also supported the hypothesis of 'alienation', stating that leading researchers consider this behaviour as child abuse. I was astounded. I knew Mal did not like me but I was incredulous at how much he hated me, and he had used the girls' emotional wellbeing with such disregard. The court ordered that the week-on-week-off arrangement be reinstated immediately.

The first time the kids came back, they were so angry at me and Cam, saying, 'Why did you take us to court?', 'We don't want to be here!' and 'You don't even love us!' Clearly resentful they were being made to come back. Things did eventually settle down and the routine was okay for a while.

As the girls got older, Pip became a loner at school, with few friends and heightened anxiety. She enjoyed her job that Cam helped her get at the local Gelati shop and studied hard at school. She loved to read and draw. I saw this as an escape from her troubled world. She also loved singing. She spent a lot of time in her room. Her moods did oscillate between happy, laughing, and interested, to uncommunicative and insular. She was just a teenager trying to find her way, hugging me one minute then scowling at me the next.

Millie was talkative and easy going; she had many friends, loved school, and socialising. Cam and Millie were particularly close, always laughing and joking together. Millie also was the one who had the confidence to answer back and argue her point of view. She also loved attention and couldn't sit on the couch without lying on Cam, or me, or both! Even though she was getting bigger, she still loved nothing better, if she was feeling unwell, than to be tucked into a bed on the couch, still with her teddy bear 'Chocolate'. They were both crazy about their dog, Pepper, too, he equally loved them too, always so excited to see them.

Mal's passive-aggressive behaviour escalated greatly at this time. I know he refused to believe the doctor's diagnosis and had no intention of considering her suggestions to improve the situation. I am sure he was very angry at me for instigating the legal action, which was directly responsible for the disparaging report.

I had planned to take the girls for a holiday to Byron Bay during the second week of school holidays. I was so excited to be having a holiday with them. Then Mal took them to Byron Bay on the first week of the holidays. Obviously, it was his intention to ruin my holiday by taking them there first, so by the time they went with me they would already have seen and done everything.

Our home life unravelled completely with one argument regarding a trip the girls were taking with Mal to Thailand. Mal was refusing to give me details of the flights or accommodation. Pip was flying back earlier for school, so I offered to pick her up from the airport, but she wouldn't give me any details and refused my offer, saying she would make her own way home or get a friend to pick her up; she was sixteen at the time. I told her I wouldn't let her go if she was coming home alone and I wasn't picking her up. Pip started yelling and stormed upstairs. Then Millie started screaming at me saying I had no right to stop them from going. They said they could do whatever they wanted and didn't have to listen to me and that they didn't even want to be here. Millie ran upstairs yelling she was going to ring Mal to come and pick them up so they could to get out of here. I went upstairs and Millie said, 'Dad's coming to get us'. I said, 'Well you better pack everything you need, then,' and went back downstairs. A few minutes later, the girls stormed out the front door with their bags. I watched them leave with Mal through the window. Neither girls have slept here since.

Mal continued to ignore the court orders, giving the impression that he is not beholden to follow the law or suggestions made by the family psychologist. My barrister made the comment that he often sees fathers like Mal. During the case, he said, 'He will never back down and will always oppose you. His narcissistic nature will never allow him to see the situation any other way but his.'

It's now been two years since I've spoken to Pip. She did answer my call once but after I said 'Hi, it's Mum!' she hung up. I did try sending messages, ring, and email for a while, but she never replied. I also offered her my car when I bought a new one, but she didn't take it. She responds to contact from my parents but never from Cam or myself. I can see what she is up to on social media and Millie fills me in with some details. I know she is happy. She has finished school and is studying design. A whole new world for her; she is free to define herself; however she wishes. I don't want to push her to see me. I know in time she will have a better understanding of it all. I've watched her struggle to keep her head above water for so long. The backwards and forwards of separate houses, trying to please both me and her dad. The utter exhaustion of constant warring parents, so all I can do wait, give her some space and time.

Cam and I do see Millie, not as often as we would like, though. Sometimes, it takes her weeks to respond to my messages or phone calls. When we do see her, she is happy, engaging, funny, and affectionate and she is very social with her friends.

I feel like Mal stole my whole experience of being a mother. He robbed me, Cam, and the girls of time together, time that can never be regained. The girls could have had a wonderful life, with two loving parents and two loving step-parents. He has stolen from them a happy half of their lives. The adventures and memories Cam and I could have contributed have been obliterated because of his jealousy. He has cost us everything and taken away such a big part of his children's childhood. The most inexplicable part about it is that he clearly and calculatedly set about to do so. I am at a loss to explain how his mind works, that he could be so neglectful of Pip and Millie's emotional wellbeing. That he would lie and make up untruths to disparage me to the girls. What sort of father tells his children that their mother doesn't love them, that it's not her fault because she has a mental illness, specifically a narcissistic disorder? What sort of father is so controlling that he is willing for his daughters to have an almost phobic-like anxiety towards their mum?

I did eventually find out Mal set up a trust account a couple of years before he left me. I assume that when he decided to leave, he systematically went about syphoning money to make sure he had enough to finance his new life. I remember telling Mal when he was leaving, 'The kids are going to carry this with them for the rest of their lives,' and he said, 'No, they'll be fine in a couple of months, they'll get over it.' I am sad that it isn't true. I am also amazed their step-mother Kim saw what was going on and didn't get involved. She read the psychologist report and knew Mal was consciously trying to turn the girls against me. As a step-mother, she also has a responsibility to protect their welfare.

These days, I don't feel like going out because I don't want anyone to ask about the kids. People don't know what's happened so I am sure they automatically think I must have done something wrong if my kids don't want to see me. I have been very lucky to have Cam by my side. His support and love have been my lifeline. I know he is also devastated with the way everything transpired. He loves the girl's and misses them so much, too. It is heartbreaking that the girls don't seem to remember what it was like; all the fun we had and the times we spent together. It is strange looking at such happy times in photos and all the girls tell me was they were always miserable, and I was never there for them.

Some nights I stay up. It is peaceful and calm, but there is an undertow of sadness and longing, something missing. Then I remember the girls aren't asleep in their rooms and aren't here with me. Then I remember why, and I am overwhelmed with anger, hurt, and outrage.

I am not sure if they will ever understand what has happened, or how much I love them and have suffered by not having them with me. I have to hold on to the fact that I will never give up on them, I believe in them and hope their lives are happy. I think of them every day and dream of them every night.

I wish them love, I wish them happiness, I wish them health. I wish their dreams come true.

LEGAL COMMENTARY

There were clear signs of family violence in Fiona's relationship, which include emotional and financial abuse, which was identified by Fiona's GP following the separation. There is a clear difference between separation-instigated family violence, which is brought about at the time leading to the separation, and coercive and controlling violence, which shows an established pattern of behaviour. From Fiona's description, the family violence had taken place in the period following Millie's birth.

Unfortunately, Fiona didn't seek legal advice until years after her separation. Even though Fiona and Mal were not married, Fiona was entitled to a financial property settlement, and interim financial support, and should have sought advice about these issues immediately, particularly given the clear concerns around the family finances, and the fact that Mal was effectively managing her business, and his own. One of the first steps undertaken by a lawyer at this stage of a separation is to request disclosure of each party's financial position, including a copy of any bank accounts and business documents[15]. This should have been done to identify what had transpired with the family income during the relationship and to ascertain whether there were any liabilities that Fiona may have been exposed to through Mal's actions during this time.

Fiona may have been able to access jointly owned funds to pay her lawyers, which is often called 'security for costs'. Underlying this concept is the fact that both parties are entitled to financial support and legal advice, and that the federal courts have jurisdiction in such cases, even if parties were not married.

Fiona asserts that Mal was sent letters 'over the next few years' by her lawyers seeking to finalise the parenting and financial aspects of their relationship. But there were ongoing issues during this time with school fees and rent for Fiona, and it appears that she did not receive the benefit of ongoing financial support. Arguably, this should have been dealt with by legal action.

Mal did not have the authority to change the children's school without Fiona's consent. This should have been addressed at the time by Fiona, through legal action, if necessary. It is important to note that even if there are no parenting orders in place following separation, both parents automatically have shared parental responsibility for their children, which means they have an equal say regarding education, health, religious, and welfare issues. This clearly encompasses the schools that children should attend[16].

Fiona describes receiving a barrage of text messages and tirades from Mal, six years after their separation, which again highlights significant concerns regarding his behaviour pertaining to boundaries. The fact that he had her under surveillance is otherwise extremely concerning and suggests that she and the children were at risk. This could have been addressed by a warning that an intervention order would follow if the behaviour continued, and by Fiona seeking an intervention order for her protection.

An intervention order, in my view, is a powerful tool which can have the impact of correcting such behaviour, knowing that, if a breach of the order should occur, Mal could have been imprisoned.

A further issue that needed to be addressed promptly by Fiona and her lawyers was the significant travel the children were undertaking when they relocated to reside with Mal's mother, an hour away. This could have been a trigger for the parenting arrangements to be changed, and Fiona could have sort as part of those proceedings that the children remain with her during the week.

Mal's hatred of Fiona was uncovered by the family report writer once proceedings had commenced. If this process had commenced earlier, then arguably, significant damage to the children could have been moderated or reduced.

Legal Commentary by Monica Blizzard Accredited Family Law Specialist (LIV)

Suzie

Mother of two sons, Hudson and Joel

Profession: Hairdresser

Location: Melbourne, Victoria

'You'll never know dear how much I love you,
please don't take my sunshine away.'

- Paul Rice

I once lived in a fairy tale, a magical whirlwind romance filled with excitement. We fought then made up, fought then made up, at least ten times a week; he flirted with other women but somehow made me feel special; he compared me to his two ex-wives but assured me I was 'The One'. As I walked down the aisle to marry this man, I was overjoyed, he had chosen ME to heal his broken dreams. I would love and nurture this poor man who had been hurt by so many people in the past.

In 2001, the love of my life arrived in the form of a beautiful, whopping, nine-pound baby boy, Hudson. In front of family and friends, Dillon was a great father; busy changing nappies and being an adoring playful dad and husband. Mums would comment about how lucky I was, complaining their husbands were always too tired to help. Little did they know it was all a facade. Nevertheless, this was the person I chose to marry, and I was determined to make it work.

Unfortunately, Dillon had little faith in the institution of marriage as his biological father left when he was a baby, his stepfather left when he was a teenager, and his first two wives had affairs with family members. He had huge abandonment issues, so I wanted to smother him with love and security. It seemed, however, that no matter what I did, it was never enough. The battles and mind games within our seemingly happy union were never-ending.

In 2004, three years later, Hudson's brother and best friend arrived: baby Joel. From day one, this gorgeous, innocent, little soul was the apple of his brother's eye; Joel consuming Hudson's every waking moment. Even in later years, when they spent time apart because of school, Hudson couldn't wait to see his brother at the end of the day, and the feeling was mutual, it was beautiful to witness. After Joel was born, my attitude toward our marriage changed. I had become increasingly frustrated, because everything I did was never good enough. I was juggling my sons with my business (a hairdressing salon), luckily, with the love and support of my devoted parents and best friend, Lisa. My parents, 'Nan and Pop' had a strong bond with their grandsons; Pop was Hudson's best mate. Their favourite outing was fishing down at the pier or sailing on their boat. Pop also spent time with boys; at the beach, in their pool, or playing cricket and football. Joel was Nan's 'little man'. They loved singing, dancing, drawing, and watching Spongebob together. Both my sons would nag me constantly to stay at Nan and Pops, they loved being with them. I was so proud to have two wonderful sons who brought Mum and Dad so much joy and happiness.

My best friend, Lisa, was always (and still is) there to pick up the pieces. Whether I needed a loving 'aunt' to watch my sons, a counsellor to unjumble my scattered thoughts, or even a hand with the housework, Lisa was there to help along with her children (my godchildren) Tommy and Lola.

Ten months after Joel was born, two significant events occurred: Lisa's second baby, Lola, was born, and I left my husband for the final time. The arrival of Lola made me realise how precious life is, and the people around me. I was suffocated in a hurtful, toxic marriage which prevented me from being the best mother, daughter, and friend I could be.

Dillon used his charm and manipulation on many of our family and friends, causing them to believe my father and I were the ones treating him badly. They soon realised the truth when none of his stories ever added up. I was fortunate to have the love and support of Dillon's brother, Marcus, his wife, Paige, and their children. They had endured past incidences with Dillon which had led to major family breakdowns. When faced with Dillon's ultimatum, 'If you ever speak to Suzie again, you're no longer my brother', Marcus simply replied, 'My loyalty lies with my nephews, not you, not Suz. I will always be there for my nephews.' He even called Hudson every night to wish him goodnight during the first year of our separation, because Dillon was 'unavailable'.

Two years later, our lives took another significant turn when two girlfriends and I decided to take on the Kokoda track in Papua New Guinea. It didn't take long for us to establish a relationship with our Australian guide—a strong yet gentle, charismatic Melbourne man named Francis. He spoke of the soldiers with such compassion. He taught us dates and statistics like a university professor and took on treacherous terrain like an athlete; he would even comfort us when we cried over missing our children. Francis and I continued hanging out when we arrived home and four months later, we surprisingly fell into an unbreakable bond of love and mutual respect. He had two sons of his own, which meant between us we had four sons: Hudson (then 6), Joel (3), Mitch (16), and Kevi (13). It didn't take long for my sons to see the 'big boys' as their real-life superheroes, especially Kevi. He took the big brother role by the horns: reading them bedtime stories; teaching them how to kick a footy; buying them treats from the milk bar. The boys adored him!

Together, Francis and I loved, guided, nursed, protected, and advised our four soldiers the best we could through their life hurdles, and after six years, we officially became a family when Francis and I tied the knot, in January 2014. Although it was a happy time, this was unfortunately when our nightmare began.

After we announced our wedding plans, one year prior to our special day, Hudson became increasingly uncooperative and disrespectful towards Francis and me. It was his first year of high school and he was making no effort to learn or enjoy it, which was sad because his primary school years had brought him so much happiness. Each fortnight, he would return from his father's with more disturbing comments about our parenting. Slowly, he became more distant and withdrawn, until one morning I asked, 'What will make you happy, how can I make you happy?' He sternly replied, 'I'm not going to be happy until I live with my dad!' My younger son started crying saying, 'I want to stay with Hudson.' Dillon's day of glory had arrived; he had manipulated my sons' minds with endless false promises and talk of an amazing life with him. I believed this nightmare would only last a couple of weeks, at most. I couldn't have been more wrong.

After three years and five months of living in a home without them, I can now finally see exactly how Dillon and his wife had manipulated the family law system and my sons. I believe that they were very threatened by the fact that Hudson and Joel had a loving and responsible stepfather, stepbrothers, grandparents, and extended family. During this time, the trauma and alienation we've endured are as follows:

Francis had a six-month Apprehended Violence Order (AVO) put on him, with many false allegations consisting of physical and emotional abuse. This AVO was in place prior to our wedding which was intended to prevent my sons from attending. They did attend our wedding as our lawyer at the time had added a clause that if my sons wished to attend our wedding, they could. They were petrified to notify their father of these wishes, so I simply told them to tell him after the wedding. It took about twenty minutes after the ceremony for them to melt into Francis' arms and realise that he was not angry, he just missed them terribly.

- Francis and I had supervised drug testing for three months. My ex-husband and his current wife were ordered to take the same tests, but they didn't comply; there were no consequences for them.
- We had full police checks into drug dealing.
- Francis was threatened that he'd be reported for severe child abuse which could cause his employment of twenty-five years with the fire brigade to be terminated.
- We were accused of drink driving offences, and drunk and disorderly.
- We were accused of continuously stalking and threatening Dillon, his wife, and their other children, an eleven-year-old daughter, and sixteen-year-old son who was taken by the DHHS because of severe neglect and abuse six years prior, and her nineteen-year-old daughter who was raised by the grandparents for various reasons.

After all these investigations were proven false, the bombshell came and almost destroyed my parents' health and our family's sanity. Dillon accused my father of sexually molesting Hudson. It started off as one small false allegation and with each interview with the police unit, Sexual Offences and Child Investigative Team (SOCIT), and Hudson's psychiatrist, the story was changed to the point where it was actually a joke.

My father, who is a most respectful father and grandfather in his mid-seventies, had endured the worst nightmare. He was interrogated for over ten hours (over two separate visits) and investigated by police and DHHS in their family home. The investigation was closed after six long months, and when asked why it took so long for an outcome, we were simply told, 'As this was not a severe case where the child was in immediate or severe danger, it had basically been put on the 'back-burner''. This traumatic period in our family's life, especially my father's, was certainly far from 'not severe'. As this was the first time any of our family members had had any police involvement, it rattled all of us to the core. After the case was closed, Dillon and his wife, again, suffered no consequences for wasting police and DHHS time and resources.

Shortly after these allegations were put to rest, I found myself in a position where I had to make a serious decision to choose life over the alternative. A very unfortunate incident stopped me in my tracks but forced me to evaluate our whole heart-wrenching existence. I'd had a very heated argument with Hudson's psychiatrist on the phone. He had nervously told me that he was well out of his depth and he could not help my son anymore, as he couldn't determine who was telling the truth. This sent me over the edge in an instant; I was a severely desperate mother clinging onto whomever and whatever I could to help my sons out of this horrible prison. I had learnt of this latest psychiatrist through the court documents; Dillon had formed a pattern of changing my sons' therapists every time I had contacted them and informed them of the severe alienation and manipulation.

This argument landed my husband and I in the back of an ambulance with a slash to my wrist and deep wounds across his fingers where he snatched the knife from me. I had finally snapped. I honestly do not know how this happened; it was almost an out-of-body experience, and like a 'strobe' effect. One minute I was on the phone, and the next my best friend Lisa was hugging me in hospital. The surreal moments in between were feelings of extreme panic, confusion, and anger. I was staring death in the face. I just could not handle any more doors being slammed shut. My ex-husband had successfully manipulated not only my sons against me, but also anyone who had any authority in deciding what was in the best interest of my sons.

My ex-husband and his wife were experts in dealing with family law matters and DHHS. They'd had previous experience as they'd had two children removed from their care and both had had numerous dealings with Victorian Police. They had learnt how to 'walk the walk and talk the talk' (a little phrase a lawyer had used during a meeting). She also informed me 'off the record' that truth, unfortunately, has NOTHING to do with it and I needed to learn how to 'play the game' just as Dillon and his current wife had.

This hospital visit, and the realisation that I really was not coping as well as I thought I was, and the fact that I had dragged my family and close friends down with me, led me to the decision to leave it to fate. We could not have fought any harder than we did; we tried absolutely everything we could to both defend ourselves against the continuous false allegations and to protect and rescue my sons from their father's toxic prison. All we were doing was just fuelling their fire and filling the pockets of the seemingly-useless lawyers that were supposedly fighting to return my sons back to me. We just could not physically, emotionally, or financially take any more.

In my heart, I knew that my sons would find their way 'home'. They were raised with a solid foundation of unconditional love, guidance, encouragement, and support. They were taught respect and the importance of truth. During my darkest days, I struggled severely with thinking, Where did I go wrong? I eventually found comfort in the thought that, It is what is it, somewhere, somehow, my sons and I had some very important lessons to learn.

Almost three years after not laying eyes on my sons (except from a distance in court, and the back of their heads when they refused to look at me during mediation sessions), Hudson is safely back in my arms! I cannot describe the feeling I had when he ran across the courthouse, emotionally calling, 'MUM!!' It was the same incredible feeling I had when the doctor gave him to me at Sandringham hospital almost sixteen years prior. He was the most amazing gift anyone could have given me, and I've been so blessed to have received him twice! Incredible!

Unfortunately, the circumstances in which he was returned aren't at all pleasant. The DHHS, police, and hospitalisation of Hudson was involved, BUT he not only survived, he gained so much strength and wisdom, and so much more than any textbook could ever teach him. The biggest one of all is what kind of father and husband he DOESN'T want to be. He learned the hard way for himself that unfortunately, his father wasn't the superhero he thought he was. He also discovered that love and acceptance from family should not come with rules and conditions; a real family has a strong, unconditional, unbreakable bond.

I, myself, have learned some extremely valuable life lessons too. Amongst many other things, patience and gratitude are of extreme importance. My patience was pushed to its absolute limit, but somehow, I found peace in 'it is what it is' and one of my precious sons is back home with me. My patience will help Hudson, my family, and I remain strong and focused until the time is right for my youngest son Joel to return safely back with us. I've always loved and appreciated my nearest and dearest, but I am so COMPLETELY in awe of the beautiful souls who've nurtured me in their unconditional love, no matter how difficult this horrendous ride got.

Eight months down the track, we are neckdeep in court proceedings again, trying to bring Joel home where he is loved and missed by so many, but we are all embracing this precious solo time with Hudson. It's been an incredible journey watching him regain the sparkle in his eye, the passion to live, and a much needed six or so kilograms (I can't believe how much teenagers eat!).

So here we are, filled with unconditional love, patience, gratitude, strength, wisdom, and HOPE. Joel will find his way back 'home' … Just as Hudson did … Just as your beautiful children will, too.

LOVE AND TRUTH CONQUERS ALL.

LEGAL COMMENTARY

From Suzie's story, the apparent trigger in an escalation of behaviour from Dillon was her marriage to Francis, and the formation of their new, blended, family unit. It appears the alienation with Hudson coincided with his commencement of secondary school and the children's 'disturbing' comments seem to be the first indication of the damage to their relationship with their mother. Suzie should have sought specialist family law advice at the time that her sons started making these comments. This advice may have led to her seeking child inclusive mediation to understand the source of the change and strong wishes from Dillon, or it could have led to court proceedings and a family report, which may have exposed what was occurring between them at that time. If sought early enough, a family report can be a powerful tool in detecting parental alienation.

Suzie suggests that Dillon was able to manipulate the family law system, in addition to the children, to achieve their goals. It is true that an intervention order, or an 'AVO' (Apprehended Violence Order), which is a term used in some states, can be used as a weapon rather than a sword. Allegations in an application for an intervention order are made in a written application in the first instance, and then by giving verbal evidence in the witness box. There is typically no opponent when the order is made, so the court only hears one side of the story. This means that the court will, in many cases, make the interim order, which means that unless the defendant attends court to defend the application, it can thereafter be made on a final basis[17] . In this case, it appears that the target of the accusations was not Suzie, but Francis.

It appears that Suzie and Francis were subjected to multiple false allegations. When allegations around drug use are raised, one way to defend such an application is by voluntarily providing supervised drug screens or a hair test which will show whether drugs have been detected. If a positive test is made, then this could lead to supervised time with the children being ordered. If no positive test is found, then often the accusations can be found to be baseless. Accusations regarding criminal behaviours, such as drink driving offences, and being drunk and disorderly can be disproven by issuing a subpoena to the police. Allegations regarding stalking and threats can be proven or disproven in multiple ways. One way is by obtaining records to show your location at the time of the alleged incident, whether by social media apps, CCTV or telephone records, or otherwise by giving evidence, or having witnesses give evidence on your behalf.

Allegations of sexual abuse can be a sinister weapon in legal proceedings generally, as the court is likely to act protectively and provide for supervised time in a reflex action, leaving the allegations untested until an interim defended hearing, or a final hearing can take place, which can be twelve to eighteen months later. When dealing with allegations of this nature, a lawyer can prepare by providing a psychological assessment of the accused, and character witnesses in their support. But the risk to the child is so concerning, that even in those circumstances, the court may order supervision, or limited time with the children and the accused, until the final hearing stage.

One of the most concerning elements of Suzie's story is the assertion that Dillon changed his sons' therapists every time she contacted them to inform them of the manipulation. In that respect, Suzie's lawyers should have intervened to ensure that the children would not be exposed to too many professionals. This is something we often refer to as 'systems abuse'. It is not clear whether this issue was raised, or how the court tolerated such a significant change in the psychological supports for the children.

In this case, thankfully, Hudson was able to find his way back home. Part of this may have been due to his age. At sixteen years of age, the court would be likely to take his wishes into consideration and Dillon would have had substantive difficulty in resisting his wishes.

The incident referred to by Suzie, which involved the police, DHHS, and the hospitalisation and any evidence from Hudson himself which could be provided by way of a counselling or psychologist's report, could be persuasive evidence, which could assist Suzie in returning Hudson's brother, Joel, home again.

Legal Commentary by Monica Blizzard Accredited Family Law Specialist (LIV)

Hudson

Son of Suzie, brother to Joel

Profession: Student

Location: Melbourne, Victoria

'Know your parent for who they are not what your other parent says they are; make up your own mind.'

- Hudson

My mum and dad broke up when I was four. The only memory I have of them together was when I was in between them while they were fighting, and they didn't notice I was there. I also remember sitting on the porch outside the front door waiting for Dad to pick me up, but sometimes he wouldn't arrive.

Things didn't really change when I got older. I never felt like I was Dad's favourite; we didn't really talk much because we didn't have much in common. The only thing that seemed to please him was when I said bad things about Mum and her family.

He used to take me to see psychologists to talk about everything and before we'd walk in, he would coach me on things to say like, 'I have nightmares about Pop touching me and doing 'things''. He also took me to the police to tell them the same story, there's a whole coronial file about it, but there was never any real evidence, because nothing ever happened. He would also say things like, 'If you DO say Pop has done 'that', we will go through the court process a lot quicker, you just need to say IT.' I did, and that was what stopped us from seeing Mum, which is exactly what he wanted.

After a while, our disagreements became more intense, often turning into fights and not just with me and him, the whole family was getting involved. Then one time, Dad snapped to the point where he head-butted me, then punched me in the nose, and in the side of my head, and after that one, I blacked out.

To explain how bad the brainwashing was in that house, the whole time we were fighting my younger brother, Joel, was saying, 'Why are you disrespecting Dad?'

I thought I was beyond the point of return. I thought Mum would hate me if I came back, I thought Pop would hate me if I did. Which wasn't true, they knew what was up the whole time.

Only after several physical fights did DHHS finally decide to return me to my mother. It took me to be beaten black and blue for this to happen. I will never forget the joy in my mother's eyes when the judge said I could go home with her; we hugged tighter than I've ever hugged someone before. I am one of the lucky ones, though, who had the chance to right the wrongs I did, not continue to live constant lies and be in fear of my life at home. I can only hope my younger brother can find his way back to us too, one day. I think about him all the time and miss him more than words can say.

If our story is something you relate to, don't waste another day in fear, tell someone what is happening and give your other parent another try, even if it's been years since you've been in touch, if you don't try you'll never know.

After almost three years apart, I now live with my mum, step-dad, and two step-brothers. I was reunited with my Pop, but unfortunately, nine months later, he passed away after he lost his battle with a rogue rip while swimming with my Nan off the shore of Nauru.

PART TWO

UNDERSTANDING
BEHAVIOURS & THE LAW

SURVIVAL RESPONSES

FIGHT, FLIGHT, FREEZE OR SUBMIT

All mammals, including adults and children, are evolutionally designed to respond in one of the four following ways when faced with a threat:

- Fight: This person responds by stepping towards the threat to try and overpower it.
- Flight: This person will attempt to flee the threat, physically or psychologically.
- Freeze: This person cannot fight or flee and so the best way to survive is to shut down physiologically and mentally, like the opossum, which will 'play dead'.
- Submit: This person feels helpless and powerless, so the best way to survive is to seemingly give in and go along with the person or situation that is a threat.

If you have a child who is in 'fight' mode, you might think this is a child who is really naughty. They may, for example, bully other children or be defiant. This is not because they are bad or horrible, but because they are struggling with what they are experiencing and are trying to find the best way to manage it. The 'bad' behaviour is the child reenacting the dynamics being experienced at home. On the other hand, you might have a child who is in 'submit' mode. This child may be passive and unresponsive. This child may have difficulty making friends, participating in the classroom, and potentially be subjected to bullying by other children. Teachers may not recognise the child in submit mode is having difficulties because they are not causing trouble.

ATTACHMENT TO THE PERPETRATOR

Children have two basic survival needs. Firstly, they need to attach to their caregiver(s) for food, shelter, safety, emotional, and mental development. Secondly, children need to withdraw from a threat to protect themselves. The child in an abusive, neglectful, or chaotic family is caught in a double-blind, with two opposing survival needs. Firstly, the child needs to maintain attachment to their caregivers. Secondly, he/she needs to defend him/herself from those same caregivers, who are meant to offer protection. Children have no capacity to defend themselves physically or to protect themselves emotionally or mentally. Invariably, a parent is not abusive all the time. Episodes may come and go, which leaves the child in a constant state of tension, trying to anticipate what they will be faced with when they get home. Will it be 'good' mummy or daddy or 'bad' mummy or daddy?

To maintain survival the child needs to develop a range of defences. Dissociation of unacceptable feelings and experiences allows the child to maintain attachment and mask deep, inner conflict of both love and hate for the abusive parent(s). This behaviour can set the stage for destructive attachment and relating patterns later in life.

TRIANGULATION – KARPMAN'S 'DRAMA' TRIANGLE

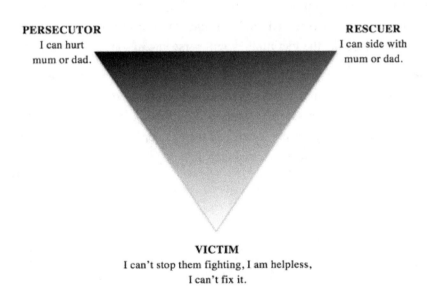

PERSECUTOR
I can hurt
mum or dad.

RESCUER
I can side with
mum or dad.

VICTIM
I can't stop them fighting, I am helpless,
I can't fix it.

When a child finds themselves in a family environment where there is a lot of turmoil, a triangle effect occurs. The triangle reflects a conflicted relational dynamic. Once the triangle has been activated, the players in the dynamic will bounce from one point to another. The triangle can play out between two, three, or more people; parents, children, counsellors, lawyers, teachers etc. It can also play out internally within the individual, whereby external circumstances or internal thoughts, feelings, or sensations can activate the triangle and see the person playing out all points of the triangle in how they relate to, and treat, themselves.

The Victim: is overwhelmed by their own sense of vulnerability, inadequacy, powerlessness, and helplessness. 'I can't fix this, you fix it for me.' Please note: The term 'victim' in this context does not refer to a person who is being victimised: abused or traumatised. If someone is being hurt by another person or situation, they are a victim. The victim in the triangle dynamic refers to a person projecting responsibility onto others to rescue them. Of course, in the case of children, they do need adults to protect them.

The Persecutor: is unaware of their own power and how they are using it in a negative way. The persecutor's internal perception is often that they are the one being persecuted, and that they are the victim. So, to enable them not to feel like the victim, they will persecute in some way or another

The Rescuer: seeks to try and save those who they perceive as vulnerable and unable to take care of themselves. This, in turn, makes the rescuer feel powerful. The rescuer is often perceived by others, in particular by the victim, as being the persecutor because the rescuer 'takes over' and often imposes their will on the perceived victim.

© 2018 Naomi Halpern

A CHILD CAUGHT BETWEEN PARENTS

Anyone can find themselves caught up on the triangle and invariably we will all experience it at different times in our lives; at work or in a friendship group, it can flare up in any situation. The task of each player on the triangle is to recognise what role they are playing and to find a way to step off the triangle. If a child is caught in this dynamic between warring parents, they will feel:

- Bad things happen to me because I am bad (thinking of themselves as losers) (Victim).
- I am bad because I do bad things (e.g. by telling lies or hurting one parent in response to the other hurting them) (Persecutor).
- I am all-powerful and I can fix it (they are in the middle, trying to keep the peace) (Rescuer).

A child or adult can find themselves bouncing around each point of the triangle in an attempt to defend themselves. If they feel victimised, they will respond in some way to make themselves feel like they have some power. This will often be in an unreasonable way; therefore, they will become the persecutor. Being unreasonable will cause the child or adult to feel bad: the victim point of the triangle becomes activated. Thus, the players on the triangle become caught in a never-ending cycle.

STEPPING OFF THE TRIANGLE

Once the triangle is activated, it is always the parent's responsibility to own their part in the dynamic and find a way to step off, so the cycle doesn't continue to perpetuate. The parent may need to seek help to do so: counsellors, mediators etc. It is never the child's responsibility to 'fix it'.

LEGAL STRUCTURES

THE FAMILY LAW SYSTEM IN AUSTRALIA

For many, the family law system in Australia is confusing. This may, in part, be due to the many issues that appear to be covered by this area of law, which include:

- Divorce and separation
- Children's and parenting matters (including relocation applications and complex litigation)
- Property and financial matters (including complex property settlement litigation)
- Spousal maintenance (married and de facto)
- Binding financial agreements
- Consent orders
- Family dispute resolution (Section 60I Certificates)
- Family violence and intervention orders
- Multi-party disputes (including corporate entities, and grandparent applications)
- Superannuation splitting
- Injunctions and restraining orders
- Child support agreements, child support applications and adult child maintenance
- Lesbian, gay, bi-sexual, transgender, intersex, queer, asexual+ (LGBTIQA+) related family law matters
- surrogacy, donor agreements and adoption
- International children's matters (including child abduction)
- Paternity.

There are both state-based courts (Children's Court of Victoria and Magistrates Court of Victoria), and federal courts (the Family Court of Australia and the Federal Circuit Court) operating within the area of family law. In general, the federal courts deal with the majority of issues that arise from separation, including property settlements and parenting disputes.

111

The state-based Magistrates Court can, in certain circumstances, also deal with such matters. The state-based Children's Court typically deals with applications concerning children and young persons at risk and is categorised as follows:

- The Family Division deals with the protection and care of children and young people, including applications relating to children who may be at risk; and applications for intervention order matters;
- The Criminal division deals with criminal offences of children and young people.

If there is a parenting dispute, the state-based courts may have jurisdiction over and above that of the federal courts. Two examples of this are:

1) Where a party has sought the assistance of the Magistrates Court for anintervention order, and urgent orders are required for parenting or property matters which are made at the same time.
2) Where the DHHS has issued an application in relation to children of a relationship through the Children's Court, seeking a protection order. Typically this is done in circumstances where the DHHS has determined that the parents are not acting protectively towards the child/ren.

THE COURT STRUCTURE IN VICTORIA AUSTRALIA

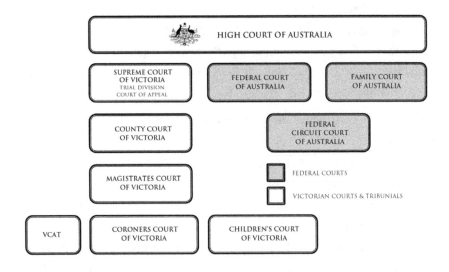

FAMILY COURT OF WESTERN AUSTRALIA

Western Australia has its own Family Court. If you are in Western Australia or your case is proceeding in the Family Court of Western Australia, you should call 08 9224 8222.

Visit this website for information on each Australian state and territories courts: http://www.familycourt.gov.au/wps/wcm/connect/fcoaweb/contact-us/locations/

THE LEGAL PATHWAY FOR A PARENTING CASE

The Family Law Court of Australia (FCA), and the Federal Circuit Court of Australia (FCC) are the first points of entry for those wanting to resolve matters relating to their separation, including parenting arrangements.

Before issuing proceedings in a parenting case, the law requires you to have first made a genuine attempt to resolve the matter by way of family dispute resolution (FDR) or mediation. This requirement is subject to certain exceptions, including cases of urgency; where the court is satisfied that there are reasonable grounds to believe that there has been, or there is a risk of, abuse or family violence by one of the parties to the proceedings; an order has been made on that issue in the previous twelve-month period; or a party is unable to attend FDR due to remoteness of their location or an incapacity[18] . The court requires a party to file, together with their court application, a certificate from an FDR Practitioner, known as a Section 60I certificate.

A section 60I certificate can be issued on a number of grounds including the following:

- An assessment by an FDR practitioner that 'it would not be appropriate' to conduct or continue FDR.
- Where a party has failed to attend FDR due to the refusal or failure of the other party to attend.
- Where the parties did attend but were unable to resolve the dispute.
- That the parties attended but did not make a genuine attempt to resolve the dispute.

Before attending mediation, you should obtain family law advice from a family law specialist to understand your legal position. This will enable you to genuinely try and resolve your dispute before having to engage lawyers on an ongoing basis to negotiate on your behalf or commence legal proceedings. Lawyers are otherwise obliged to advise you of alternatives to resolving your dispute, other than litigation, which includes mediation.

In a family law case, such as a parenting dispute, the powers/jurisdiction of the Children's Court can be invoked if the Department of Health and Human Services (DHHS) determines that it may be necessary to do so for the protection of a child. The DHHS may become involved in the following circumstances:

- By way of a formal notification being made to the DHHS directly about the risk to a child and any subsequent investigation;
- By way of a Notice of Risk form being filed by a party to a proceeding, which is a document which must be filed in any parenting application and which specifically relates to a child being exposed to family violence, or abuse/neglect, or at risk of being exposed to family violence or abuse/ neglect .

As part of a court application on parenting matters, the parties must file a Notice of Risk, dealing with potential risks around family violence, abuse, and neglect[19] . Once the court application is filed in a parenting matter, the Notice of Risk is served upon the DHHS. This means that even if a notification has not previously been made to the DHHS, they may intervene in the proceedings, of their own right, if they deem such action necessary for the protection of a child.

In the event that the DHHS does intervene in the family law proceedings, the family law case is suspended (and the Federal Courts have no jurisdiction) until such time as the DHHS investigation or State-based Children's Court proceedings are finalised.

In order to avoid the DHHS intervening in your particular case, you need to ensure that:

- You comply with any recommendations of the DHHS;
- You are seen to be placing the needs of your child above all else and are acting 'protectively'.

In my experience, the DHHS workers are often overworked, and under-resourced. The impact of this is that they usually will not intervene in cases where parents are seen to be complying with their recommendations and are acting protectively, leaving the parenting arrangements to be dealt with by the Federal Courts, or by the parents directly via negotiation. In cases that do proceed in the Children's Court, expert legal representation is strongly recommended from a specialist family lawyer.

PARENTING ORDERS IN THE FEDERAL COURTS

When making parenting orders in the FCA or the FCC, the Court must have regard to the matters set out in the Family Law Act 1975 (FLA). In particular, the court has regard to two primary considerations, which are:

1) That children benefit from having a relationship with both of their parents (section 60CC(2)(a));

2) The need to protect children from physical or psychological harm and from being subjected to, or exposed to, abuse, neglect or family violence (s 60CC(2)(b)).

In the event of a conflict, the court is required to give greater weight to the need to protect a child as the primary consideration (section 60CC(2A)). The court will then look to additional considerations in making parenting orders, which are set out in Section 60CC(3) of the FLA. They include:

- any views of the child
- the nature of the child's relationship with each parent and others (including grandparents and relatives)
- the levels of cooperation between parents
- the likely effects of any changes in the child's circumstances, including the likely effect on the child of any separation from either of their parents, or any other child or person (including a grandparent or another relative) with whom the child has been living
- the practical difficulty and expense of a child spending time and communicating with a parent
- the capacity of each parent to provide for a child
- the maturity, gender, lifestyle and background of the child and parents (including being Aboriginal or Torres Strait Islander)
- the parental attitude towards the child and parental responsibilities
- family violence involving the child or a member of the child's family
- whether it would be preferable to make an order least likely to lead to the institution of further proceedings in relation to the child.

In case where no risk to the child is established, both parents will have an opportunity to have significant time with the child, and the parenting arrangements will vary depending on the ages of the children, the location

116

in which the parties reside (and the practicalities involved in spending time arrangements) and the commitments of the parties generally. Typically, when children are young, the focus in parenting arrangements is on spending frequent periods of time with the child (and not necessarily including overnight periods), gradually increasing to overnight periods, and then block periods, as the child ages.

In cases where shared parental responsibility is ordered to confirm that both parents have an equal say and the right to be consulted regarding long term issues (such as health, education and religion) the court will consider whether equal time is appropriate and in the child's best interests. Even if equal time is not ordered, the law requires the time between a non-residential ('live with') parent to include weekend time and time during the week. This is to enable both parents to have a meaningful relationship with their children and to participate in their education, sporting activities and also recreational time.

PARENTING ORDERS OR A PARENTING PLAN?

I am often asked to explain the difference between a parenting order, and a parenting plan and the answer is, quite simply, enforceability.

A parenting plan is a written agreement setting out parenting arrangements by two parents, for their children. It can be formed from a mediation session, or from direct negotiations, but it is only a piece of paper. It has no force and effect on its own, other than being a record of what was agreed.

A parenting order is something very different. It can be enforced by a court. It can be provided to the police, if a child is not returned. It can be provided to a school, to inform the school as to who should be collecting a child. It can be enforced by way of contravention proceedings in the family law courts, if breached. It can prevent a child from travelling overseas.

In cases where there is extreme hostility or conflict, a lack of trust, and the threat of family violence, a parenting order can be the key tool in protecting children. If parties cannot agree as to the orders that should be made by consent, then the court can make a parenting order on an interim or final basis.

A child under the age of eighteen years is typically not involved directly in the court proceedings, other than via the family report process. The Family Report can be conducted by a family consultant who is employed by the Court, or privately by a psychologist nominated by the parties, at their cost. There can be a significant difference in the quality of the reports, and in my experience, and if you can afford a private report, then this is the preferred alternative.

A parenting order provides a level of security and sets boundaries, whilst also providing stability for the children. One of the many provisions that can be included in parenting orders, is something we refer to as a 'non-denigration order'. This is an order that restrains the parties from speaking badly of one another, or allowing anyone else to do so, within the presence and hearing of the children. The aim of such an order is to prevent parental alienation, however, it is obviously difficult to monitor, other than via comments being made by the children.

SHARED CARE

It is important to note that even if there are no parenting orders in place following separation, both parents automatically have shared parental responsibility for their children which means they have an equal say (and a right to be consulted) in relation to decisions regarding a child's education and health issues, religious and welfare issues including the school at which the children attend[20] .

However, contrary to popular belief, shared care is not ordered in most cases, and in fact, is ordered in a minority of cases. In cases where shared care is ordered, typically children are older in age, the parents reside local to one another and the school, and the parents have an amicable co-parenting relationship.

KEY DEFINITIONS AND ACTION POINTS

FAMILY VIOLENCE

In 2011, the definition of family violence in the Family Law Act was expanded to incorporate notions of coercion and control (which are not always accompanied by physical violence or threats). At the same time, the definition of child abuse was amended to include serious psychological harm arising from the child being subjected to or exposed to family violence.

4AB Definition of family violence etc.

1) For the purposes of this Act, family violence means violent, threatening or another behaviour by a person that coerces or controls a member of the person's family (the family member), or causes the family member to be fearful.

2) Examples of behaviour that may constitute family violence include (but are not limited to):

   (a) an assault; or

   (b) a sexual assault or another sexually abusive behaviour; or

   (c) stalking; or

   (d) repeated derogatory taunts; or

   (e) intentionally damaging or destroying property; or

   (f) intentionally causing death or injury to an animal; or

   (g) unreasonably denying the family member the financial autonomy that he or she would otherwise have had; or

   (h) unreasonably withholding financial support needed to meet the reasonable living expenses of the family member, or his or her child, at a time when the family member is entirely or predominantly dependent on the person for financial support; or

   (i) preventing the family member from making or keeping connections with his or her family, friends or culture; or

   (j) unlawfully depriving the family member, or any member of the family member's family, of his or her liberty.

(3) For the purposes of this Act, a child is exposed to family violence if the child sees or hears family violence or otherwise experiences the effects of family violence.

(4) Examples of situations that may constitute a child being exposed to family violence include (but are not limited to) the child:

    (a) overhearing threats of death or personal injury by a member of the child's family towards another member of the child's family; or

    (b) seeing or hearing an assault of a member of the child's family by another member of the child's family; or

    (c) comforting or providing assistance to a member of the child's family who has been assaulted by another member of the child's family; or

    (d) cleaning up a site after a member of the child's family has intentionally damaged property of another member of the child's family; or

    (e) being present when police or ambulance officers attend an incident involving the assault of a member of the child's family by another member of the child's family.

PARENTAL ALIENATION SYNDROME

Unfortunately, in the family law system, there are frequent examples and reports of 'parental alienation syndrome'. This can be described as behaviour towards a child, which has the effect of influencing and ultimately damaging the relationship between the child and the other parent. Sometimes, the alienation can be forceful, and directly aimed at damaging the relationship through coercion. At other times, it can be subtle and difficult to detect—forming part of the grieving process—and comes about due to consistent denigration of the other parent. Both (and all of those cases that may fall in between) can be equally devastating for the child and the parent who is left behind to pick up the pieces. A common trigger in parental alienation cases, can be the introduction of a new partner into the family dynamic.

The prevalence of parental alienation in the context of family separation is significant, and may in part be due to the difficult transition a couple must face; from an intact family unit to separated families. I often say to my clients that one of the greatest difficulties they will face in the separation process is to disengage from their partner—in a romantic sense—and to re-engage as parents. Some make the transition well, and others, particularly those more difficult separations where there may have been a breach of trust, find the transition impossible.

Another important feature of parental alienation can be the deteriorating mental health of one of the parties, or the existence of a personality disorder. These issues can be identified by obtaining a psychiatric assessment during the proceedings.

By its very nature, parental alienation can be difficult to detect. The change in the relationship may be gradual, with erosion taking place over time. It may subside after a period of time, and repair itself, or it may become permanent.

If the court makes a finding that parental alienation has taken place, then various orders can be made to try and repair the relationship between the parent and child, ranging from family therapy to a change of residence for the child. There are cases where court intervention has been left too late, and the damage has been done.

In my experience, early detection of parental alienation is the key. Typically, the court will require independent verification of the claim of parental alienation from a third-party, or another resource, which can come in many forms, including the following:

- It can be established by evidence from the family report writer or family consultant, who has interviewed the family and assessed the child as part of a family law case. In a parenting case, the family report writer is a key witness in the proceedings, whose role is to assess and interview the family and make recommendations to the court.
- It can be evidenced by third-party professionals engaged outside of the litigation, such as a school counsellor or child psychologist engaged by one of the parents.
- It can be established by direct evidence, by comments being overheard by independent third parties who give evidence in a dispute, or by a party

placing a recording device in a child's bag, and the recording providing the direct evidence of the behaviour.

- The course taken by a court will depend on when the alienation is discovered/proved, the length of time it has been occurring, and the ages of the children at the time it has been proven. Each case is different, and the Court will often require the assistance of professionals to find a pathway forward.

Due to the specialist nature of our federal courts (FCA and FCC) and the fact that many of the judges hearing the dispute have worked in family law, often as a lawyer or barrister for some time, the signs and red flags of parental alienation may be clear. This may not be as clear in cases where a protective application has been made by the DHHS and the matter is being determined by the state-based Children's Court, due to differing experiences, different court rules, and evidentiary requirements.

If you suspect that your child has been subjected to parental alienation, you should seek specialist family law advice urgently. A specialist family lawyer can assist you to establish that parental alienation is taking place and provide you with advice as to how to deal with this through legal channels, should this become necessary.

It is not sufficient to see any lawyer. You should seek the assistance of a family law specialist. You can obtain a referral to a family law specialist by contacting the Law Institute of Victoria, and in doing so, you will be able to obtain thirty minutes free legal advice. Many lawyers will speak to you by telephone initially at no charge or offer a fixed fee for an initial consultation.

NARCISSISTIC PERSONALITY DISORDER

Families who are caught in bitter separation battles can often also be dealing with a range of mental health conditions which may have contributed to the breakdown of the relationship. These mental health conditions may include substance abuse, bi-polar, schizophrenia, and personality disorders including Borderline Personality Disorder and Narcissistic Personality Disorder. People often use terms of psychiatric disorders without understanding the criteria to meet a diagnosis and/or without an actual diagnosis being made by a psychologist or psychiatrist. It is important to be careful about the language that is used. Many people caught in custody disputes and family violence situations speak of their partners as being 'narcissistic' or that these kinds of traits become apparent when feeling threatened. Below are the personality traits that characterise Narcissistic Personality Disorder:

Identity: Excessive reference to others for self-definition and self-esteem regulation; exaggerated self-appraisal may be inflated or deflated or vacillate between extremes; emotional regulation mirrors fluctuations in self-esteem.

Self-direction: Goal-setting is based on gaining approval from others; personal standards are unreasonably high in order to see oneself as exceptional, or too low based on a sense of entitlement; often unaware of own motivations.

Empathy: Impaired ability to recognise or identify with the feelings and needs of others; excessively attuned to reactions of others, but only if perceived as relevant to self; over- or underestimate of own effect on others.

Intimacy: Relationships largely superficial and exist to serve self-esteem regulation; mutuality constrained by little genuine interest in others'' experiences and predominance of a need for personal gain[21] .

FALSE ALLEGATIONS

Drug use: When allegations of drug use are raised, the best way to defend such an application is by voluntarily providing supervised drug screens or a hair test. If a positive test is made, then this could lead to supervised time with the children being ordered. If no positive test is found then often the accusations can be found to be baseless. Accusations regarding criminal behaviours such as drink driving offences and being drunk and disorderly can be disproven by issuing a subpoena to the police. Allegations regarding stalking and threats can be proven or disproven in multiple ways. One way is by obtaining records to show your location at the time of the alleged incident, whether by social media apps, CCTV, or telephone records.

Sexual abuse: Allegations of sexual abuse can be a sinister weapon, as the court is likely to act protectively and provide for supervised time, in a reflex action, leaving the allegations untested until an interim defended hearing, or a final hearing, which can be twelve to eighteen months later. When dealing with allegations of this nature, a lawyer can prepare in advance by providing a psychological assessment of the accused, and character witnesses in their support. But the risk to the child is so concerning, that even in those circumstances, the court may order supervision, or limited time with the children and the accused, until the final hearing stage.

RECORD EVIDENCE

With the modern technology we have available via our smartphones, I often advise clients to record an incident or the aftermath of an incident, in full view of the other party, as proof of what has transpired. This can often be a key part of the case, or act as a deterrent to a party taking legal action or reporting the matter to the police. There may otherwise be CCTV available in public areas, and if there are concerns around the potential behaviours of the other party, then it is important that the location of changeover is secure.

SAFETY ACTION POINTS

Ideally, seek legal advice from a specialised family lawyer before separating from your partner.

This will allow you to:

- create a safety plan around you leaving, noting that a person is most at risk of family violence in the period immediately leading to and following separation
- ensure you have safe accommodation to move to at the time you leave which can accommodate yourself and the children
- ensure you have the children in your care, when you leave
- ensure you have access to financial information from your relationship to enable advice to be obtained in relation to your settlement
- to enable you to have the primary care of the children, pending agreement being reached as to future care arrangements.

Legal Commentary by Monica Blizzard Accredited Family Law Specialist (LIV)

RESOURCES

DO YOU NEED SOMEONE TO TALK TO?

Lifeline - 13 11 14 - lifeline.org.au

Beyond Blue - 1300 22 4636 - beyondblue.org.au

Suicide Helpline - 1300 651 251 - www.suicideline.org.au

Mensline - 1300 78 99 78 - mensline.org.au

Kids Helpline - 1800 55 1800 - kidshelpline.com.au

Child Protection Crisis Line (Vic) - 13 12 78

1800RESPECT - 24/7 (Aus) - sexual assault, family violence counselling - 1800respect.org.au

Family Relationship Advice Line (Aus) - 1800 050 321 - familyrelationships.gov.au

FAMILY VIOLENCE SERVICES

Safe Steps Family Violence Response Centre - 24/7 Call 1800 015 188 - safesteps.org.au (women and children only)

Centres Against Sexual Assault (CASA) - casa.org.au

Domestic Violence Resource Centre - dvrcv.org.au

inTouch Multicultural Centre Against Family Violence - intouch.org.au

Victims of Crime - victimsofcrime.vic.gov.au

Women's Information and Referral Exchange (WIRE) - wire.org.au

FAMILY RELATIONSHIP SERVICES

Parents Beyond Breakup (Aus) - parentsbeyondbreakup.com

Dads in Distress and Mums in Distress support services, weekly meetings.

Phone - (02) 6652 8113 or 1300 853 437

Relationships Australia - 1300 364 277 - relationships.org.au

Lifeworks (Vic) - 1300 543 396 - lifeworks.com.au

DADS, MEN AND BOYS

One in Three - oneinthree.com.au

Men's Health Australia - menshealthaustralia.net

Dads in Distress (see Parents Beyond Breakup)

Mensline - 1300 78 99 78 - mensline.org.au

Stop Male Suicide - stopmalesuicide.com

LEGAL AID CONTACTS

Victoria - 1300 792 387 - legalaid.vic.gov.au

Western Australia - 1300 650 579 - familycourt.wa.gov.au

South Australia - 1300 366 424 - lsc.sa.gov.au

Queensland - 1300 65 11 88 - legalaid.qld.gov.au

Northern Territory - 1800 019 343 - legalaid.nt.gov.au

Canberra/ACT - 1300 564 314 - legalaidact.org.au

CHAMPION WOMEN IN THIS SPACE

Karen Finch – CEO Legally Yours

www.legallyyours.com.au

Fusing together her legal background, recruitment expertise and passion for shaking up the legal sector, Karen is passionate about facilitating faster, easier and more transparent access to fixed-fee lawyers in Australia. A Legally Yours lawyer member won't send you 'surprise' invoices, they won't speak legal jargon to you, and they will always provide transparent delivery of legal services to their clients every time - guaranteed. Fast, easy, transparent!

Tanya Lavan – R.B Flinders - Family Lawyer (Collaborative)

An advocate for change in the family law industry, Tanya seeks to promote Collaborative Law and provide people with a greater understanding of the family law process. Her Instagram page @familylawtoolkit provides key insights for parties experiencing separation and she frequently posts blog posts on the rbflinders.com.au website.

Amanda Sillars – CEO Eeny Meeny Miney Mo Foundation

www.emmm.org.au

A leader in advocacy, education, raising awareness and providing resources about parental alienation. Amanda is also working in collaboration with the University of Tasmania for research on Child Abduction and Parental Alienation. On 12th October 2016, her organisations started Parental Alienation Awareness Day Australia #PAADay. Her passion is helping children and parents reunite, her social media groups and pages connect parents alike from all over the world.

Tanya Somerton – Divorce Angel

www.tanyasomerton.com

Having endured the terrifying and complicated process of divorce has created the Ultimate Divorce Experience and is now helping women survive their separations through her company Tanya Somerton Pty Ltd. With an 'Army of Angels' working together including a team of Lawyers, Financial Advisors, Counsellors, Child Psychologist, Mortgage Brokers, Life Coaches, Stylists and much more. No stone is left unturned in getting her clients the best possible outcome and framing their future success. 'Making anything possible.'

Melinda Nutting – Step by Step Support for Separated Families

www.stepbystepsupport.com.au

Specialised Family Separation Consultants who have created a 'modern, healthy' separation service providing child-inclusive and therapeutic mediation options (parenting and financial), and incorporating non-adversarial legal services in their business. They also work with court-ordered families. They utilise their background in children's counselling, post-separation parenting programs, mediation, and also as separated parents themselves. Australia-wide via video appointments.

GLOSSARY

Adjourn: To defer or postpone a court event to another day.

Affidavit: A written statement by a party or witness. It is the main way of presenting the facts of a case to the court. An affidavit must be signed before an authorised person (such as a lawyer or Justice of the Peace) by way of swearing on the Bible or attesting to the truth of the contents of the statement.

Appeal: A procedure which allows a party to challenge the decision made by a court.

Contravention: When a court finds a party has not complied with (followed) a court order, that party is in contravention of (or has breached) the order.

Consent order: A written agreement that is approved by a court. A consent order can cover parenting arrangements for children as well as financial arrangements such as property and maintenance. Any person concerned with the care, welfare, and development of a child can apply for parenting orders.

De facto relationship: The law requires that you and your former partner, who may be of the same or opposite sex, had a relationship as a couple living together on a genuine domestic basis.

DHHS: Australian Department of Health and Human Services.

Enforcement order: an order made by a court to have a party or person comply with (follow) an order.

Family violence: Violent, threatening, or other behaviour by a person that coerces or controls a member of the person's family (the family member) or causes the family member to be fearful.

Family violence order[22]: An order (including an interim order) made under a prescribed law of a state or territory to protect a person from family violence.

Family report: A written assessment of a family by a family consultant. A report is prepared to assist a court to make a decision in a case about children.

Family consultant: A psychologist and/or social worker who specialises in child and family issues that may occur after separation and divorce.

Family dispute resolution: A process whereby a family dispute resolution practitioner assists people to resolve some or all of their disputes with each other following separation and/or divorce.

Interim hearing: A hearing that looks at the issues that need to be decided in the short term, such as where the children will live.

Interim order: An order made by a court until another order or a final order is made.

Intervention order: A court order designed to protect a person by placing limits on the behaviour of another person. It can be made to protect a person from: physical assault, sexual assault, harassment, property damage, or interference with property, serious threats, or stalking, which might include: following, hanging around home or workplace, phoning/emailing/texting.

Family violence intervention order: can be made against a family member or a person you have been in a relationship with. A personal safety intervention order can be made against a person who is not a family member.

*Note: New laws have been introduced across Australia so that all intervention orders (which are domestic violence-related) made on or after 25 November 2017 will be nationally recognised and enforceable. This means, wherever your order is issued, it will apply in all states and territories so that you are protected wherever you may be in Australia. If you have an intervention order (domestic violence-related) issued before 25 November 2017, and you would like it to operate nationally, you can apply to any court to have your order declared. To read more about the national domestic violence order scheme go to www.ag.gov.au/ndvos. If English is not your spoken language, you will find information in a number of other languages at on www.ag.gov.au/ndvo

Note: A breach of an intervention order can result in the perpetrator being jailed. This threat can be a powerful influence in curbing bad behaviour from one party.

Mediation: Divorce mediation is a process that allows divorcing couples to meet with a specially-trained, neutral third-party to discuss and resolve common divorce-related issues. Mediation is typically less stressful and less expensive than a divorce trial, and it usually proceeds much faster.

Parental alienation: (see description in legal notes)

Parenting orders and parenting plans: (see description in legal notes)

Post-natal depression (PND): is depression occurring in the months following childbirth. The onset of PND tends to be gradual and may persist for many months and even years. Some parents feel ashamed if they are not coping and so may try to hide their struggles. Signs and symptoms can vary but usually includes feelings of shame, guilt, failure, inadequacy, hopelessness, tearfulness, and persistent low mood.

Recovery order: A court order directing or the Australian Federal Police (AFP) to take all appropriate action to find, recover, and deliver a child.

Reunification (RT): is a therapeutic intervention for separated families when the children find difficulty visiting with the noncustodial parent.

Subpoena: a document issued by a court at the request of a party, requiring a person to produce documents and/or give evidence to the court.

Supervision order: gives the local authority (police) the legal power to monitor the child's needs and progress while the child lives at home or somewhere else. A social worker will advise, help and befriend the child. In practice, this will mean they give help and support to the family as a whole[23] .

ENDNOTES

1   Family Law Act 1975 Section 22 (2) (b)

2   Australian Bureau of Statistics 2013, U.S.A Census Bureau 2012.

3   Section 4AN of the Family Law Act 1975 (Cth)

4   Section 60CC(2(a)), (3)(b)(c)(ca)(f)(i) of the Family Law Act 1975 (Cth)

5   Section 60CC(2), (2A) of the Family Law Act 1975(Cth)

6   Section 4AB, and 60CC(3)(j)(k), 60CF of the Family Law Act 1975 (Cth); Family Violence Protec-tion Act 2008 (Vic)

7   Section 61D, 61DA of the Family Law Act 1975 (Cth)

8   Section 60CC of the Family Law Act 1975 (Cth)

9   Section 65DAA of the Family Law Act 1975 (Cth)

10   Section 13C of the Family Law Act 1975 (Cth)

11   Section 62G of the Family Law Act 1975 (Cth)

12   The legal admissibility of recorded evidence will depend on the State of Australia in which it is obtained, and the manner in which it was obtained. There are sanctions, including criminal sanctions in relation to obtaining such evidence unlawfully. In Victoria, pursuant to the Surveillance Devices Act 1999 (Vic) "a person must not install use or maintain a listening device to "overhear, record, monitor or listen to a private conversation where the person is not a party to the conversation, without the consent of each party to the conversation". A recording may be admissible however, if a party to the conversation makes a recording in the knowledge, or with the consent of the other party/ies. The Family Court can allow recording evidence, into parenting cases, pursuant to Section 138 of the Evidence Act 1995 (Cth) in circumstances "where the desirability of admitting the evidence outweighs the undesirability of admitting evidence that has been obtained in the way the evidence was obtained" or if it deems that the evidence is necessary within its general discretion to determine what is in a child's best interests.

13   Section 67Q of the Family Law Act 1975 (Cth

14   Family Violence Protection Act 2008 (Vic)

15   Rule 12.02, Chapter 13 Family Law Rules 2004 (Cth)

16   Parental responsibility means all the duties, powers, responsibilities and authority which, by law, parents have in relation their child/ren (see sections 61B to 61DB of the Family Law Act for details)

17   The process of obtaining an intervention order on an interim basis, is simplified by this taking place on an ex parte basis, however a final order if contested, may not be made until a final hearing has taken place, with both parties (and additional witnesses) giving evidence in the witness box and submitting to cross examination. A party may agree to resolve an intervention order application on the basis of an order being in place for an agreed timeframe, on the basis that it is "without admission" meaning that, the perpetrator does not admit to the allegations in the application. The parties are also able to resolve the matter by; the victim withdrawing the application altogether and there being no order, or otherwise by agreeing to a legal undertaking. This is in effect a "legal promise" to the Court, which whilst not enforceable in the same way as an order, is taken seriously by the Court if it is subsequently breached.

The Law Library Victoria - https://www.lawlibrary.vic.gov.au/legal-research/courts. 2019

18   Section 60I Family Law Act 1975 (Cth)

19   Section 69Q, 67Z(2) or 67ZBA(2) Family Law Act 1975 (Cth);

20   Section 61C Family Law Act 1975 (Cth)

21   American Psychiatric Association, Narcissistic Personality Disorder - Diagnostic and Statistical Manual of Mental Disorders. DSM-5 © 2013 (latest edition)

22

23   Government of Australia, Australian Family Law Act 1975 Section 4AB, Compilation No. 83

Family Court of Australia - https://www.familycourt.gov.au. Viewed 2019

Victoria Legal Aid - https://www.legalaid.vic.gov.au. Viewed 2019

Children's Court of Victoria - https://www.childrenscourt.vic.gov.au. Viewed 2019

Government of Western Australia Department of Health - https://ww2.health.wa.gov.au. Viewed 2019

Government of Western Australia Department of Justice https://www.correctiveservices.wa.gov.au. Viewed 2019

South Australia Police - https://www.police.sa.gov.au. Viewed 2019

ABOUT OUR SPECIALIST CONTRIBUTORS

The Honourable Alastair Nicholson, AO RFD QC

Admitted as a barrister and solicitor of the Supreme Court of Victoria in 1961 and signed the roll of Counsel of the Victorian Bar in 1963. He was appointed Queen's Counsel in 1979, a Justice of the Supreme Court of Victoria from 1982-88, and the Chief Justice of the Family Court of Australia and a Justice of the Federal Court of Australia from 1988 until his retirement in 2004.

Monica Blizzard – Family Law Specialist (LIV) - KHG Lawyers

www.khq.com.au

An Accredited Family Law Specialist with the Law Institute of Victoria, delivery of legal services to their clients every time-guaranteed. Fast, easy, transparent!

Naomi Halpern – The Delphi Centre

delphicentre.com.au

Over thirty years' experience working with complex and developmental trauma, Naomi provides consultation and training for mental health professionals, government departments, law firms and the United Nations.

MEET THE AUTHOR

 Karen is a producer, author and child rights advocate, with twenty years of professional experience in the film and television industry. In 2013, Karen embarked on her first solo feature documentary Dad which was shown in Parliament, Canberra, mid–2015 as part of a Senate inquiry into our family law system. 'I couldn't believe this worldwide problem was buried so deep, one which affects people, young and old and is detrimental to our future, the cornerstone of society – family.' Karen's second project, resource Mum's the Word has brought together legal and medical specialists, parents, advocates, and young people to deliver a handbook for Australian families navigating separation. The book will educate, provide alternative solutions, and guidance through our complex judicial system. Karen hopes that by giving young people like Hudson a platform to communicate their experiences, it will urge parents to make better decisions about the adults they want their children to become.

I wouldn't be doing this if it wasn't for my mother, father, sister and husband Chris, their unconditional love, support and encouragement for this crazy career I have chosen and to our beautiful son George, I can't imagine life without him, why should any loving parent have to?

From all the mums, dads and young people involved, we thank you for your support.

CPSIA information can be obtained
at www.ICGtesting.com
Printed in the USA
BVHW041423100619
550610BV00014B/808/P